THE RIGHT WAY TO
START YOUR OWN BUSINESS

THE RIGHT WAY TO
START
YOUR OWN
BUSINESS

Rodney Willett

RIGHT WAY

Typeset in 11/12pt Times by Letterpart Ltd., Reigate, Surrey.

Printed and bound in Great Britain by Cox & Wyman Ltd., Reading, Berkshire.

The *Right Way* series is published by Elliot Right Way Books, Brighton Road, Lower Kingswood, Tadworth, Surrey, KT20 6TD, U.K. For information about our company and the other books we publish, visit our website at www.right-way.co.uk

To Marcia

CONTENTS

INTRODUCTION

This book is intended to help readers to start a business without falling into any of the more common pitfalls that trap so many who start off with high hopes, only to end up disillusioned and, often, very much poorer.

One problem is that 'business' covers such a wide range, both in terms of activity and size. Is it possible to write a book that will be equally useful both to the person who wants to run a one man business and to a group of people who intend to set up a business involving a dozen or so employees with a potential turnover of over half a million?

I believe the answer is 'yes' – but only if my readers are prepared to accept that not all that will be found herein applies to them. Accordingly, I would ask you to be patient when you come to passages designed for someone else.

Having said that, the basics are the same, no matter what you intend to do, and no matter how small or how large your proposed organisation. If you can find the time and energy to read those sections which, on the surface, appear to apply to others rather than yourself, I believe you will find the effort well-rewarded. At the very least it will give you a good idea of how larger businesses operate – and some of your customers may be larger businesses, who knows? This understanding could well help you to sell to such concerns simply because you can identify more closely with them and with their problems.

This book follows over twenty-five years of experience in running small businesses – some highly successful and one total failure – including over ten years acting as a consultant assisting, amongst others, those starting out to produce strategic and/or business plans to provide the framework for their efforts and, in many cases, to provide support during the early years.

Over that time I have discovered that running a business is not just a matter of sales and financial control, the two subjects most people consider. A business is about people – about those who start it, their customers, their employees and their other business contacts. It is about integrity, thought, decision making, humour, despair, exultation and self-discipline. Accordingly, I make no apologies for those sections which deal exclusively with people for, in my opinion, they are the most important.

Although I have considerable experience, I do not know all the answers (nor do I know anyone who does). At intervals throughout the book I shall suggest that you go and talk to someone. One of the secrets of success is to pick as many brains as you can and to hear what people have to say – some of it will be wise, some stupid, some right and some wrong. It is your job to sift the wheat from the chaff and take and use what will help you, discarding everything else.

However, at the end of the day, it is your business. Within a very short space of time you will know more about it than anybody else. Learn to trust your own judgment and remember that taking a wrong decision is often better than taking no decision at all. Take advice by all means – especially technical advice – but do not let others persuade you to do something which deep inside you feel is wrong for your business. For example, you are considering some move. You may be in doubt as to the tax implications following this move and you visit an accountant (your own if you use one) to find out exactly what they are. Some accountants (not all, that would be unfair) will also offer you advice about other aspects of your project. This is not based on real knowledge – if you have done your homework properly, you will know far more about your proposed move than that accountant.

Treat this book in much the same way. Read it with care. Think about what it says. Take from it that which is of use to you and reject that which is not.

Good luck with your new venture.

1

FIRST THINGS FIRST

Introduction

Running your own business can be the greatest adventure of your life, offering you infinite satisfaction – or the worst possible nightmare, giving you nothing but pain and worry. It is unlikely to fall in between. Whether it becomes the great success of your dreams or a total and dismal failure is up to one person – you!

The purpose of this first chapter is to help you identify whether or not you should be starting a business at all. Later, we will consider which sort of business would best suit you.

Rule One: No matter how many untruths you may tell other people, you must never, never tell any to yourself, no matter how much that hurts.

Tom and Kate decided to start their own business. Tom is highly qualified and was in a well-paid job in line for further promotion with little doubt as to his future security. His work meant that he and Kate saw little of each other because, such is his character, he would almost always bring work home. He is a perfectionist; prone to becoming irritable when matters are not going well for him. As you would expect, tension built up in the family; eventually to an extent that they felt something had to be done.

They decided to look at ways and means of moving to the country and starting a business of their own. Their intention was to create a slower lifestyle so that they could enjoy the countryside and each other's company. They chose an area where they had enjoyed many holidays, an area of great natural beauty where the general economy depends to a large extent on the tourists and visitors who arrive in their thousands each year.

In due course they sold their house and bought a property in a country village in the area they had chosen. Because house prices were higher in the town that they had left, they were able to buy a larger house with a very small mortgage. It seemed as though they had everything on their side. Kate learned a craft skill before they moved and they started the business, Tom learning from Kate as they went along. Sales were slow to begin with, which they expected, but it did not take them long to discover that the maximum they could earn (always assuming that they had a full order book) was still less than the amount they needed if they were to live as they wanted to live. As a result, Tom has had to return to using his old skills (but on a self-employed basis) in order to supplement their income.

Tom is still the same Tom and Kate is still the same Kate and so the same problems still face them. To make matters worse, they have added another difficulty: they are having to struggle to make ends meet and they have discovered how they hate being poor. The whole thing has become a nightmare.

The problem was that they created a picture of the new lifestyle that they wanted to create and peopled it with a Tom and Kate that just didn't exist. They took the decision while they were on holiday, relaxed and removed from their day-to-day selves: very different people from the Tom and Kate at home. With hindsight they now know that they should have planned the business which, if that planning had been carried out properly, would have revealed that the potential profits were not enough to meet their needs. They should have considered their skills to see whether or not they were the right people to be running a small business. Tom, coming from the sheltered environment of the employed person, finds the strain of running his side of the business very great indeed. He has difficulty in charging a fair price for his work, often doing more than he agreed to do out of a sense of guilt. This is not uncommon. If an employee is paid, say, £10 per hour to do something, the customer is probably paying over £20 per hour because of the additional costs involved in running the business. Tom is able to relate to the amount of money he was paid when employed but unable to relate to the amount his employer charged the customers. The result is that he consistently undercharges – much to Kate's fury who feels that he both could and should be making a higher contribution to their income. Meanwhile, Kate's side of the business continues to plod along but Kate is working on her own instead of with Tom as she had planned. The result is two very unhappy people struggling to make sense of life.

What sort of people *are* happy working for themselves? There is no simple answer to that question as it is made up of a number of factors. Let us look at some of them.

Motivation
Tom and Kate decided that their prime concern was to reduce tension within the family. They thought they could achieve that aim by creating a slower pace of life with time to be able to enjoy the countryside and time to be together.

In fact, as became obvious in a fairly short period of time, they had no great desire to 'enjoy the country' on a full-time basis although they had done so happily when on holiday. Now they drive past some of the most spectacular scenery without even seeing it. It has become commonplace, a part of their daily round, and so no longer special. Now it is the towns that Kate misses and she delights in being among the crowds in the shops – just what she used to be able to do on a daily basis before they moved and so, because it was then commonplace, did not value.

Their motivation was all wrong – and they misjudged that motivation because they had not been brutally honest with themselves.

So, the very first question to ask yourself is, 'Why do I want to do this?'

There are many acceptable reasons for starting a business but they must include one essential desire – the desire to succeed and that means to make enough profit to maintain your chosen lifestyle.

Some people believe that they have a far higher earning

potential running a business than they do as an employee. They are aware of their skills and expertise. They know that there are people who would want to buy their services – at prices that will make them the income they want.

Others have a need to prove themselves to themselves. They believe they could do the job better if they were their own boss, free from the controls and constraints of being employed.

Some feel that they would be more secure in business than when employed. They see their employment at risk, either as a result of redundancy or of the employer ceasing in business, and fear that their entire income may disappear almost over-night. They prefer the concept of relying on their own abilities rather than other people's.

Obviously, that list is not conclusive. However, there is a common factor. All are considering starting out on their own for a positive reason – be it greater income, greater freedom to express themselves or greater security.

Those who see a business as a way of avoiding certain aspects of employed life that they dislike are almost certain to fail. Many people are really running away from something or other (usually themselves) but they have created other, often non-existent, 'motives' which blind them to the truth.

It is impossible to give a formula to help you decide on your personal motivation. All that can be said is that you should think long and hard and, as I have already indicated, be absolutely honest with yourself.

You

In order to be successful, a business has to be a sensible project carried out by sensible people. What is a sensible person in this context? For the moment let us ignore technical matters and consider character. Character is vital for success in business.

The first aspect is tenacity – the ability to stick to a job regardless of how depressing, seemingly pointless, unpleasant, soul destroying and painful that may be.

The second is energy. I have heard it said, 'He always manages to be in the right place at the right time. It never happens to me.' The reason is usually the same. The first person is energetic – the second idle. The energetic man improves his chances of being in the right place at the right time by being in as many places as he can during the time available to him (and making as much time available as possible).

The third, integrity, is an essential ingredient. Your word should be your bond. That does not mean to say that you should never strike a hard bargain; but once you have struck a bargain you should stick to it – even if that proves to be to your disadvantage. It goes even further than that. In most businesses the businessman knows a good deal more about the matter in hand than the client. That does not give the businessman the right to make profits out of the client's ignorance. Unfortunately, integrity is not the commonest of characteristics amongst business people – witness the need for the Financial Services legislation to protect the public from unscrupulous insurance and investment salespeople. The stupid thing is that the really high performers (in every field) are those who have integrity which enables them to build on their success thanks to the reputation that they acquire. In business it really does pay to be honest – in the long term if not the short.

We all live in a world of change and that means those who will make a success of business will be those who can react to change. In simple language, that means being able and willing to learn and to go on learning. There is no room in the modern business world for those who are fixed in their ways and unwilling to give consideration to new ideas. As good a name as any for this characteristic is 'mental flexibility' and it is essential.

The last characteristic I will mention here is a never failing sense of humour. Although not essential, it certainly helps.

In later chapters we shall be looking at other personal requirements – skills, experience and more characteristics – some of which may well apply to the founders of the business.

Personal Satisfaction
It is true to say that most people carry out their 'best work' outside of their gainful employment. It happens that one of my loves is boating, and boats generally have featured large in my

life. I shall always remember two boats in particular as both were to traditional design, beautifully built and finished, the larger having taken seven years to complete. Both were built by amateurs in their spare time – one by a hospital administrator and the other by an accountant. I came to know both quite well and neither was happy in his job. They often talked about setting up as boat builders but neither was prepared to take the risks involved. I felt this was a shame because, in my experience, if someone starts a business doing something they really enjoy, the odds are that they will master everything required to make the venture a success. Furthermore, that enjoyment will result in a sparkle which will attract customers and encourage them to put their faith in the business.

True enjoyment comes not just from doing the job but from the rewards that come from doing a job well. That is critically important in a world where more and more emphasis on quality and personal service is demanded, and rightly so, by customers.

Your Family
The effect of the business on the other members of your family and the degree of support that they would be willing and able to provide must be considered.

Running your own business is always demanding and sometimes the demands will push you to the edge of your abilities. Inevitably these will be at critical moments and the support, lack of support or, even worse, actual antagonism from the family can make or break a business at such times.

Every businessperson will make mistakes and take wrong decisions. If your spouse reacts by blaming you and pointing out how stupid you have been, the effect may be to undermine your confidence in yourself – and that will do nothing but make it harder (if not impossible) for you to retain enough self-confidence to behave effectively.

Likewise, it may be that an erratic income will create problems. Not everyone can cope with uncertainty. Worry and fear are strong emotions and can make people react in a way which is far from useful or sensible. When orders are few and far between and life looks grim as the bank balance dwindles and the bills mount up – so does the pressure. These are the times for cool heads, hard work and economy – not for nagging or reacting to fear and worry by becoming extravagant (a surprisingly common reaction). The first reduces the effectiveness of the person doing his or her best to resolve the problems – the second makes the problems larger.

In addition to psychological support, you may need more practical support. If, for example, you intend to work from home but will be away for periods during the day, other members of your family may well be answering the telephone. If they answer a call from a client or potential client then, as far as that caller is concerned, they *are* the business. What they say, and the way in which they say it, can have a profound effect on the success of the business. If there are young children in the household they should not be allowed to answer the telephone. A worried person trying to find a plumber to sort out a leaking pipe might be amused to be answered by a five year old who puts the telephone down and shouts, 'It's a woman with a leak. She wants Daddy to poke something in her hole.' This happened to an elderly acquaintance of mine who thought it very funny. Others may decide to put the telephone down and try someone else.

To Sum Up

The first step is to carry out an honest and detailed personal assessment. The purpose is to ensure that your reasons for considering starting a business are positive, to ensure that you have what it takes to run your own business, that you will receive support from your family (if you have one) and that you would gain enjoyment and personal reward from the business of your choice.

Given all the above, you can have confidence in creating a worthwhile and profitable business.

2

WHICH BUSINESS?

What is a Business?

At first sight that looks like a remarkably silly question but it is impossible for us to investigate anything unless we first thoroughly understand what it is that we are studying.

A profitable business is any activity which utilises any combination of equipment and skills in order to produce goods or services which it is able to sell into a market place at a price greater than the total cost of production.

This definition identifies the main elements needed to run any business: equipment, the skills needed to produce the goods or services (which I call 'service skills'), a market place, the skills needed to sell into that market place (sales skills) and the overall ability to produce a profit. We cannot investigate the market place until we have decided on the business we intend to start. As that decision will be linked to skills and equipment, we will consider those first.

Service Skills

Most people start a business which uses the service skills they already possess. However, whilst it is a nonsense to consider starting, say, a business as an electrician unless there is a qualified and experienced electrician available to carry out the work, it is just as nonsensical to consider starting such a business unless there is work for the electrician.

A craftsman who lives in an area where there is a shortage of his craft may well be able to start a business with no need for an intensive sales campaign. All he would need to do would be to let people know he had started the business (a few cards in a few windows, an advertisement in a local paper and some striking sign writing on his van or car) after which, if he is good at his job, he may well find he has more work than he can handle as satisfied customers recommend him to their friends.

Life is rarely as simple as that and, to succeed, each business must have its own 'unique selling point' – something that makes it different from everyone else. Our craftsman has an in-built USP – he is available where others are not. So long as he continues to provide good workmanship, good service and does not price himself out of the market (which means controlling his costs), his future should be secure because others starting a similar business in competition have the problem of displacing him. (In passing, it is worth noting that many established businesses are easily displaced. This is because they become complacent and cease to provide good workmanship and good service or start to over charge.)

Almost certainly you will not need any help in deciding whether or not you have the skills and character needed to provide the services. The easiest test is to answer, honestly, the question, 'Am I good at my job and do I enjoy doing it?', where 'job' means the provision of the services you have in mind.

Sales Skills and Characteristics

What sort of person should be providing the sales? Roughly one person in four has the makings of a good salesperson – and many of those are presently doing something totally different.

Jeanne and Herbert Greenberg run an employment agency and have been involved in recruiting and training sales personnel for many years. Some years ago, they decided that it was necessary to identify the sort of person who would succeed in sales and, as a result, they spent four years carrying out a research programme in which they interviewed and analysed between 250,000 and 350,000 salespeople in the United States. Their findings are of great significance.

'It takes a special kind of person to succeed in sales. First of all, salespeople have a different way of looking at the world. They sense opportunities where others fear rejection. Frowns are not signs of discouragement, they are something to be changed. Where others see obstacles, salespeople see challenges.' *(Creating Sales Team Excellence* by Jeanne and Herbert Greenberg, published by Kogan Page. Although this book is now out of print, you might be able to borrow it from your local library.)

What do they mean by a special kind of person? First of all, the Greenbergs identify four basic characteristics (they call them inner dynamics – something inside which creates a driving force) which are needed to a greater or lesser extent in all sales situations.

The first is **Empathy**. This is the ability to read the reactions of other people, to know what they are thinking even when they are saying something rather different. Empathy can be confused with sympathy and this must be avoided. It has been said that, 'Empathy is placing yourself in someone else's shoes: sympathy is putting them on and feeling them pinch.' The empathetic salesman remains his own man with his own identity and with his own objectives clearly in mind at all times. The sympathetic man merges his identity with another and their objectives become his objectives.

Empathy is important because prospects offer many objections which are rarely valid but are used (often without realising it) to mask the real reasons for their concern. Dealing with the objections will not further the sale – that can be done only by dealing with the real reasons behind the objections.

The Greenbergs call the second **Ego-Drive**. This is an inner drive which compels the salesperson to make a sale on a personal basis which has nothing to do with cash rewards. Simply put, it is the inner need to hear other people say, 'Yes' – and it really doesn't matter what they are saying yes to.

People strive to gain personal, inner rewards. This is best explained by another quote from *Creating Sales Team Excellence.*

'Engineers are gratified by designing complex equipment, building bridges or planning a dam. Artists achieve gratification by expressing themselves creatively. Teachers achieve through the accomplishments of their students. Carpenters, tailors and repairmen achieve gratification by exercising their craftsmanship. In the same way, top salespeople enhance their egos through persuading others, frequently in a face-to-face, one-to-one situation.'

I can add from my own experience that technical writers gain their satisfaction from taking a complex subject and presenting it in a readily understood and readable format.

The amount of Ego-Drive required in a given sales situation varies widely. The salesperson who needs to make twenty sales every week requires a very high Ego-Drive – the salesperson who needs to win two or three contracts each year needs far less; indeed, a salesperson with a high Ego-Drive in such a position would suffer high levels of frustration. However, all salespeople need some Ego-Drive if they are to be successful.

Service Motivation is the third requirement. This is the desire to please – to hear someone say 'Thank you' or 'That was a first-class job.' Running parallel with Ego-Drive, it is easy to confuse the two even though they are essentially very different.

The person with Service Motivation but no Ego-Drive is likely to come within an inch of achieving a sale but then fails because of an inability to say, quite simply, 'Please sign here.' The person with Ego-Drive but no Service Motivation is far more concerned with making the sale than in ensuring that it is in the interests of the potential customer. Whilst this may produce more sales in the short run, and matters little if repeat business is unlikely, in most cases the damage that this does by creating dissatisfied customers outweighs all else.

The last major requirement is **Ego-Strength**. This is the easiest to understand – it is the inner strength needed to be able to withstand rejection. Every salesperson will face rejection. It is rarely a personal matter (the prospect may well have no need of the product or service on offer) but the person with low Ego-Strength will take all rejections as personal and soon cease to operate effectively.

Now is the time for some more brutal self-honesty. Do you or do you not possess these qualities? If you do, in what measure do you possess each?

Sales or Service
With the above in mind, you should now be able to decide on which of the following options is the one for you.

To provide the sales and look to others to provide the service.

To provide the service and look to others to provide the sales.

To provide both – which places a firm limit on the size of the business (and that may not be a bad thing).

Some additional input may help you to decide so we will look at various 'skill combinations'. Remember, however, you should not consider starting a business which means that you will not enjoy your work: that spells disaster.

If you are happy working at your craft and decide you would make a poor salesperson, you will almost certainly decide to provide the service and rely on passive selling (such as advertising) or, if need be, employ a salesperson. Your craft skills will determine the sort of business that you run unless you are prepared to attend some sort of training in a different craft (or in an allied trade so as to be able to extend the range of services that you can offer).

If you are a craftsman but you do not enjoy that work and you have identified yourself as being a potential salesman, you should give consideration to starting a business to provide a service using your craft skills but for you to sell and to employ others to carry out the work. This is a very common situation and has many advantages. You will be able to sell with authority as you know the business. By the same token you should be able to control your workers and you would be able to take your coat off and work alongside them if need be.

If you are happy as a craftsman *and* identify yourself as being a potential salesman, you have the choice. Further, you are in the ideal position to run a 'one man band' and that has a lot to commend it as you do not have to worry about relying on other people. (Although you may find it helpful to employ people to carry out simple work, you would not be relying on them as they can be replaced fairly easily. As soon as that ceases to be true, you are no longer running a 'one man band'.)

If you cannot identify a service that you would enjoy providing and you do not see yourself as a salesperson, you should not be reading this book and you should certainly not be considering branching out on your own.

Alone – or Together

From the above, you should be able to determine the sort of business that you want to start but there is one other fundamental matter to consider.

Will you run the business on your own or will you join with others?

You may well feel that you are the right person to provide the service element and you have a close friend who is also thinking in terms of a business who would make a first-class salesman. Do you employ him? Does he employ you? Do you join forces?

There is no hard and fast rule. Later we shall be looking at the various ways in which more than one person can form a trading entity and we shall see that there are no real problems associated with joining forces so long as it is done sensibly.

The decision will be taken on personal rather than technical grounds. First and foremost: do you both (or all) trust each other? Do you respect each other? Do you have confidence in each other's abilities? Do you get on? Can you disagree without the argument becoming fruitless and acrimonious?

If the answer to all those questions is 'yes', then there are advantages in the group system. Each will have given areas of responsibility and each will be equally motivated to succeed. Illness or other absence is less critical to the well-being of the business and 'two (or three or four . . .) heads are better than one'.

If you do decide on a joint arrangement, all planning should be carried out jointly. It is during that phase that you will discover whether or not your trust, respect, confidence and friendship are sufficiently well-founded to stand the strains of working together.

Other Skills

In addition to the skills needed to sell and provide your services, a range of other skills is required. However, none of these is critical to the well-being of the business as it can be bought in as required. For example, every business needs to keep its accounts in order, as we shall see in a later chapter. However, there are book-keeping services available to assist the smaller business and, as it grows, it may find there is a need to employ a full-time accounts clerk. Either way, the business can run even though the founder has no book-keeping experience.

Equipment

Every business relies on some equipment although it may be very simple.

Under this heading goes any building required, essential fixtures and fittings, essential furnishings, essential equipment and essential tools.

I have repeated the word 'essential' because so many people who come to our consultancy produce lists of requirements which include many items which are not. Some will be needed rarely and can be hired when wanted, others are of no real use other than to provide status which is not needed when a business starts. Its status will result from the quality of the goods and services supplied – not by putting expensive furniture surrounded by pot plants in the reception area.

We often have to liaise with our clients' accountants and I have had to visit two recently. Both turned out to be first class but there was one striking difference. In one, the offices were sparsely (but adequately) furnished. In the other, everything was very plush indeed. For example, the man I called to see had in his room his desk with a couple of visitors' chairs plus a coffee table, sofa and two easy chairs, cocktail cabinet and a host of potted plants, all standing on the sort of carpet that makes you reach for a lifebelt. Apart from anything else, this meant he was taking up twice the space of the first, and space costs money. Being privy to the accounts of both clients, I discovered that the second was charging nearly double that of the first for what was substantially identical work.

No new business can afford such luxuries and I would suggest that even an established business like the second may have far greater problems than the first in a period of recession when work falls off.

Having said that, in some businesses (a high-class hotel is a good example) the use of high standard furnishings, etc., may well be absolutely essential simply because customers will demand a degree of luxury.

List all essential equipment (as defined above) and work out how much it will cost. We shall be looking at financing businesses later – at this stage all that is needed is a rough guide as to cost so that you can get a feel of what will be needed.

If you are sure that you have the finance available (or, in the case of a tradesman, that you already have all that is required), all well and good. If this is not true, you will have to change your plans so that either less equipment is required or more finance is available.

This may not be fatal to your ambitions. I have known Douglas for nearly fifteen years. When he was in his early twenties, he decided that he wanted to own a garage servicing and repairing lorries. That was way beyond his pocket so he bought a large van and equipped it as a mobile workshop. Soon he had a flourishing business servicing and repairing cars at people's homes. From there it was a short step to employing someone to take over his round and for him to create a second. And so on.

That business continues to this day, except that he now has about twenty vans and each is operated by a self-employed mechanic who enjoys the use of the equipment plus the 'corporate image' and 'corporate marketing' that Douglas has created in return for a percentage of his turnover (a form of franchising). Douglas now owns the lorry service station he always wanted and, in addition, a transportation and warehousing company. The Group was valued at a little over £3,000,000 at the last count. From little acorns . . .

External Finance
In many cases, the cost of providing the equipment exceeds the cash available. Although we shall be looking at finance in

detail in later chapters, there are ways and means of overcoming this problem which you may care to consider at this stage.

You should, by now, have a fairly clear idea of which business you intend to start – you probably had that before you started to read this book – and I hope that you have great confidence in your ability to make that business work and become highly profitable. If that is the case and you know people with some spare cash, you might consider approaching them to see whether or not they would be prepared to assist in providing the capital that you need in return for a share in the profits. Before you ask them to make a firm commitment, you should show them a business plan (and we will see how to prepare one in a later chapter) but this does not stop you sounding them out before then. Most British enterprises of any note were started by combining certain skills (yours) with a supply of capital (theirs) so you are asking for nothing out of the ordinary. Indeed, it is a great shame that more people considering starting out do not follow this route even when the finance needed is quite small. It is infinitely preferable to taking a loan, although it must be accepted that it is not always possible.

As we have seen, you may well feel that you are the right person to provide the service element and you intend to look elsewhere for the selling skills. Do you know of someone who is also thinking in terms of starting a business who would make a first-class salesman? It could be that by joining forces – and cash availability – you would both benefit from working together.

If you want to start a business and look after the sales, the same concept applies except that you will need to find someone with the required service skills as well as some cash.

You may be able to obtain a good deal of the equipment that you require on some form of lease purchase arrangement which also reduces the capital required. Unfortunately, this is usually quite expensive (despite certain tax advantages which really only apply when you are established and profitable). Since this reduces the profitability of the business, it may not be a sensible solution. However, if there is enough profit to cover the extra costs it is well worth considering.

Lastly there are loans. This is a complex subject and is dealt with in detail in a later chapter. Assuming that a loan is forthcoming, the same comments regarding profits apply.

Taking the Decision

With the above in mind, you should now be in a position to decide what it is you want to do and have some idea of the scale of the operation.

Try not to be too vague. Write down what you plan to do – even if it can be summed up in a single sentence – and indicate what you hope to achieve in financial terms. The following are some examples.

'To set up as a plumber offering general plumbing repairs to start with and then moving on to new installations including central heating systems. I would expect to get enough sales by advertising and I do not want to employ anyone apart from a mate if that proves necessary. I want to achieve a clear income of £16,750 per annum.'

'To set up a design studio offering a design service to industry, commerce and the catering trade. Although I shall start on my own, relying on my own abilities as a salesman, I hope to see the business grow until it employs a full-time salesperson and a number of other designers. I would be content with an income of £15,000 to start with but I would like to think I can gradually increase that to about £40,000 per annum.'

'To open a retail shop selling fashion clothes to young people. The profit at the moment doesn't matter as we can live off my husband's salary but it must always cover its costs and I want it to make enough money to be able to save enough to make our old age comfortable.'

'To buy and operate a hotel. The size of hotel will be determined by the purchase price and how much I can borrow. I want it to be a seasonal hotel so that I can spend the winter carrying out refurbishment work and gradually making

*the building more valuable for when I would want to sell it
and buy something bigger. That means I want to buy something in fairly poor condition in a good tourist area. Since we
would be living in the hotel, we can manage on £11,500 per
annum.'*

*'To act as a distributor for firms making engineering
components who are not represented in this area. I should be
able to pick my suppliers if I offer commission only terms and
I would select those that I know I can sell to my existing
contacts. I would hope to make at least £17,500 in the first
year.'* (Was this an employed representative who felt he had
nowhere to go if he stayed put?)

*'We want to design and build boats to fill the market gap
which exists for small general purpose rowing, sailing and
outboard boats which can be carried easily on a car roof rack.
Tim would look after the sales, George production and I
would be responsible for designing the boats and looking after
financial matters. To make sense of it, we should have to make
a profit of £86,250 a year to divide between us.'*

3

THE MARKET PLACE

Introduction

Having decided what we intend to do, we must look at sales. Sales are absolutely critical to any business, for without sales there is no business. Some people start a business because they are enthusiastic about some particular activity (such as a sport). Unfortunately, this enthusiasm may not be shared by a sufficient number of others to support the venture. There is absolutely no point in providing a source of supply to meet a demand that does not exist.

Therefore, our next job must be to satisfy ourselves that there is a demand for our proposed business. First, we have to determine how we can investigate the market in which we want to operate; how to find out how many potential clients are in our catchment area, what percentage of those are likely to become actual clients and how much each actual client would be likely to spend.

There are two exceptions to this rule – the first is the craftsman I mentioned previously filling a known gap in the market. The second is when a person is buying an up-and-running business (one example being a car hire business) with no need to improve the level of sales (simply because the existing sales are already sufficient to meet the purchaser's requirements and their value should remain linked to inflation) – but only so long as it is a business which does not rely on the personality of the owner to maintain those sales. Some businesses, for example, a public house or small hotel, rely very heavily indeed on the personality of the owner. If you fall into either of those categories, you may wish to ignore the rest of this chapter and go on to Chapter 4.

Market Research
The tool that we use to determine the demand available to us is Market Research. This may be simple and cheap to implement – it may be highly complex and cost a good deal. It may be something we can do ourselves – we may need to call on the help of experts.

However it is carried out, this research should not only provide you with information as to what people want but also as to how much of it they want and what they are prepared to pay to get it. It should also acquaint you with details of any competition that may exist.

Do not fall into the trap of believing that a demand exists simply because there is no local source of supply. On the contrary, the lack of any local source of supply should make you consider the very real possibility that there is no real local demand at all!

Likewise, do not be put off if there appears to be a good deal of competition. The fact that there are many sources of supply means that the demand has been established. If you are then able to offer a better or cheaper supply centre, and preferably better as it is harder for competitors to lift standards than it is for them to drop prices, you will be able to create a successful business.

How you set about trying to answer the question posed above will depend entirely on the sort of business that you are considering.

The concept behind all market research is simple – putting it into practice is not and, unless you have virtually unlimited funds available, the costs may be prohibitive.

Consider a firm planning to build a new supermarket. The investment will run into many millions and so a good deal of money will be made available to ensure that the investment proves profitable before any plans are finalised. How do they set about it?

First of all, they want to know, in terms of percentage of the population, the average number of visits made to supermarkets each year. This they may well be able to establish from their own records if they already own other outlets and it could be a figure such as 1,250 per cent (25 per cent of the population visiting 50 times per annum) or even higher.

Secondly, they will want to find out what distance people are prepared to travel in order to visit a supermarket. This will vary widely depending on many local factors – they will be seeking to find the national average.

With those two facts before them, they can establish the 'catchment area population' for the proposed supermarket: the total population who live within average travelling distance of the proposed site. By applying the 'visit factor', they can estimate the number of people who would pass the check-outs each year.

Now they need to know something about the competition. How many supermarkets are there in or near the catchment zone which will have an effect on the proposed supermarket? This is easily established. More difficult is to quantify that effect. However, let us suppose that they decide that only 30 per cent of the catchment population is exposed to competition and that they expect that 50 per cent of that 30 per cent would continue to use the supermarkets they presently patronise. This means an adjustment to predicted customer base.

However, competition comes from other shops, not just supermarkets. This is why the calculations have been based on average figures since this additional competition will be fairly standard throughout the country. A survey will be carried out in the locality to check that there are no special factors to consider – special factors which may cause adjustments to the predicted customer base either way.

In this case the next question is probably the easiest to answer. What is the average spend per visit per customer? They will almost certainly be able to answer this one from their own existing records.

From this data they will establish the predicted gross sales and so the net operating profit. If this is high enough to justify the expenditure, they will proceed. If not, they will think again.

That is, of course, a fairly simple model and overlooks a

number of complications but it does give an idea of how market research is carried out. The difficulty is that it all depends on two factors – average conditions in the industry and a knowledge of the population in the catchment area. Although this covers selling to the general public, the same concept applies when considering selling to other businesses.

How does that help us? It may be possible to determine industry averages by approaching trade associations. A visit to the bank is also worthwhile as most high street banks keep statistics which they may be willing and able to make available although, now most branches have been demoted to the status of a sub-branch, you will almost certainly have to go to the area office to find someone who can help you. Whether or not your bank will have the figures you want is a matter of luck. A further source of assistance may be major suppliers in certain sectors. For example, brewers should be able to assist if you are considering starting out in a pub. If none of these approaches works, you are very much on your own.

Somewhat easier is to determine the magnitude of the target market. Businesses generally fall into one of two categories: those where the customers come to the business to place the order and those where the business goes to the customer to get the order.

In the first category, the size of your target market will be a percentage of the local population. The size of the local population can be found by contacting the records office of your local authority. The percentage which applies to your proposed business is far harder to determine. The classic method is simple: ask a large enough sample to provide an accurate picture. Unfortunately, that is easier said than done. For one thing, it takes a good deal of experience to know how to word questions so that the answers provide the required information and how to ask those questions so that the answers are not distorted. One problem is that most people like to be helpful – and they often answer questions the way they think the questioner wants them to rather than absolutely honestly. If you can afford it, you can consider employing a market research agency. If not, this method is probably best ignored as you are likely to end up with wrong information which is worse than none at all.

In the latter case you need 'positive selling' and can sell wherever you like (subject to financial constraints). The size of your target market will not be infinite but may be considered so in certain cases.

To see how, and if, this helps in practice, we will look at the six examples quoted at the end of the last chapter.

The Plumber

Many businesses are started offering one of the trade services by an experienced tradesman.

In some cases, the business is started because the tradesman finds himself made redundant or the firm for which he works ceases to trade. In such a case it is essential that the reason behind the redundancy or closure is understood. It may be that the employer was having difficulty in finding enough work. In that case, is there any reason to believe that life will be easier for the new business?

Our plumber could try to carry out some market research as outlined above but he may have problems. For a start, his ambition to become involved in fitting central heating systems poses a problem. It is extremely unlikely that there are any records showing what percentage of properties (either nationally or locally) have had such systems fitted in recent times. His own observation will tell him whether or not his locality is mainly older properties (either without central heating or with out-of-date systems due for renewal), new properties with modern systems or a fair mix of the two.

Having said that, since he has been working in the area in which he proposes to start the business (which is usually the case), he already has a good deal of local knowledge. Is it possible to use that to create the statistics needed? There is one method which works quite well which he might try. He buys a pack of small record cards and writes on the top line the names of as many customers visited in the last couple of years as he can remember. To start with, the names come quickly and then the pace slackens. However, if he keeps at it he will find names coming almost out of the blue until he has a respectable pile of cards to work with. Now he moves on to the second phase. (If this is done before all the names have been remembered, the number of names will be fewer which is why the two jobs should be tackled separately.) Phase two is to record on each card as much about the plumbing in each house as he can remember.

Done properly this will provide the basic percentages required and will be automatically right for the area. This exercise should give a good idea of the number of properties with existing systems and the number of those systems that should be due to be replaced. (Incidentally, instead of using cards, you may prefer to put the data onto a computer and we shall look at that possibility later on.) Furthermore, the cards may well reveal possible plumbing needs (which, since the people will know the plumber – unless they have moved – should be followed up). These cards should provide other statistics, too. What was the average size of job? What was the average number of hours spent on each job? All this comes from existing local knowledge but some sort of framework is required to make sense of it.

Looking at the competition is also useful. How many businesses are there in his area which offer a service comparable to the one he proposes? Are they busy? Are the owners reasonably prosperous? Are people generally satisfied with the service that they get? Do people have to wait to get what they want? Do they feel that they are paying too much for the service?

By asking questions and keeping his eyes open, the plumber should be able to get a general feel of the position. Remember that the plumber is not interested in establishing the total demand – all he needs to check is that there is enough demand to keep him busy.

The Studio
This is a very different case. Although there are advantages in serving local businesses, it is possible to provide this facility on a nationwide basis. Indeed, modern communications and the facility to attach files to emails (a subject I deal with in detail in Chapter 16) means that long distance working has never been easier or as competitive.

With all art oriented projects, the USP (Unique Selling Point) is the creative ability of those involved. Since that can be rather nebulous, it is almost impossible to try to come to any conclusions on a statistical basis. Presumably this designer is setting up because he believes that he has great creative ability. In that case his best course of action is to visit as many potential clients as he can to find out by personal contact how many would be likely to use his services and what level of business he could reasonably expect from them. The larger the sample, the better.

The Clothing Shop
It is difficult enough to predict the sales of standard and classic clothing. To predict the demand for fashion items is almost impossible. It will depend in part on the area – how fashion-conscious it is and how wealthy.

Having said that, the amount of fashion clothing actually worn is a matter of observation and I am sure that this lady has already spent many hours looking at what the youngsters in her locality buy.

However, it would be foolish to proceed without discussing the proposal with some of the potential suppliers. They will know from their records the levels and patterns of spending in the various parts of the country and should be able to tell our retailer whether or not the town where she intends to open the shop takes more, fewer or the average number of garments when compared with other similar towns – similar in size, fashion consciousness and wealth. If it takes fewer, that suggests that there is a demand which is not being satisfied and that there should be room for her shop. If it takes more, that may be because the local demand is already saturated and she may be wise to think again. She should be a little suspicious of what they say. It is possible that they want to see an additional outlet for their goods and the picture they paint could then be rather optimistic. However, if you take the opinion of a number of suppliers, you should end up with a fairly accurate picture of the potential.

Since she is not overly bothered about making a profit immediately, the demand she needs to establish is fairly small to start with.

The Tourist Hotel

This is a market sector where there is a good deal of information available. All areas have tourist boards which keep records of past occupancy levels and predicted trends. They should be able to provide all the assistance that is needed.

However, it is worth looking at the previous history of the hotel he intends to buy when he has located it. The previous owner should be able to give names and addresses of all guests who have stayed over the last five years or so (although many will not). These should be analysed to see what level of repeat business has been achieved. The hotelier may decide to contact a sample and ask them what it was that attracted them to the hotel, whether or not they were satisfied, what changes they would like to see and, incidentally, whether they would be interested in coming back again.

The Engineer

In this case, I would be tempted to put the cart in front of the horse. By that I mean I would try to obtain general agreement with a number of suppliers so that I knew exactly what components I would be carrying before trying to determine the demand for those goods.

Once that has been established, the territory that will be covered must be fixed. The next job is extremely tedious: it is to find the total number of potential customers in that area – usually extracting the details from the Yellow Pages but the statistics may be available at a large central library and some county councils maintain record departments.

Again a sample number should be contacted to try to determine the percentage who would become customers and the average annual spend per customer.

The Boat Builders

Clearly this team has established that there is a gap in the market. What they need to find out is how that gap came into being.

Is it there because the demand has fallen away? Is it there because existing boat builders have concentrated on other areas and this has become neglected?

In this case the most likely source of help would be the publications which concentrate on boating and sailing. They receive many letters from readers which they are unable to print and could well be able to answer the above question.

. This is the sort of case where the businessman is generally 'flying by the seat of his pants' as no amount of research can really provide the answers. In one sense, absolutely every adult between the ages of, say, eighteen and forty-eight, could be a potential customer. The fact that they have never been in a boat in their life does not alter that fact – many people start boating with a car top boat.

To Sum Up

It is often impossible to arrive at accurate figures for demand unless a great deal of time and money can be spent, in which case it is probably sensible to employ a market research agency.

However, we rarely need accurate figures. What we do need is to be sure that the demand is large enough to support our business as well as our competitors. Even that may not be possible and we shall have to content ourselves with the best answers that we can find.

At the end of the day, most businesses are started because someone has a hunch that the demand exists. We may have to be content with that hunch but it should be as well-informed as possible.

4

WILL IT PAY?

There is little point in running a business unless there is the intention of making a profit – and yet many people start businesses which, with hindsight, they realise could never have been profitable under any circumstances.

In order to answer the question 'Will it pay?' certain assumptions and estimates will be used. These should be based on the best possible information obtainable. All sales estimates should err on the low side and cost estimates should err on the high side. That way can lead to pleasant surprises – the reverse to extremely unpleasant shocks.

Now where do we start? First of all, let us look at some definitions. *Sales*, in this context, is the total value of sales over a period of time regardless of what is being sold – otherwise known as the turnover of the business.

Almost every business will have to buy something specific in order to achieve those sales – what this is depends on the business. A cost which is specific to a sale is called a *Direct Cost*. Directs costs can be expressed as a percentage of sales. It is vital to understand this link if the business is to be costed properly and it applies no matter how simple or how complicated the business may be.

In some cases the position is obvious and the calculations are easy to carry out and to understand. The obvious example is the retailer – he buys goods he intends to sell and the cost of those goods is his direct costs.

In other cases it may look impossible to reduce direct costs to a percentage and this may be true in the short run. If you repair cars, the direct costs will cover the spare parts you use. The cost of spares supplied per hour of labour will vary but, in the long run, will be found to be a fairly consistent percentage of sales although it calls for more data and some calculation to establish the required figure.

In many service businesses, the direct costs are very small and can be ignored. A window cleaner uses (say) 10 squirts of detergent per hour and gets 200 squirts per container costing £1.80. Each hour his direct cost is 1/20th of £1.80 or 9p. As he charges £17.50 per hour, the direct cost is only 0.5 per cent of sales.

If you subtract the direct costs from sales you are left with the *Gross Profit* which is quite simply the profit made on a sale excluding all the other costs involved in running the business. (To avoid confusion, I should add that if you look at various business accounts you will often find that all or some staff costs are also deducted before the gross profit is shown. There may be good reasons for taking that position but it is almost always best to follow the normal pattern when costing a business.)

These other costs then have to be considered. They are most easily understood if they are divided into three: *Staff Costs*, *Fixed Costs* (such as rents or rates which do not vary at all regardless of the level of sales) and *Overhead Costs* (such as the telephone bill which varies depending on the level of sales but cannot be expressed as a percentage of sales). Just to reinforce that last item: part could be described as a fixed cost (the rental), part may result from selling (which may or may not result in business) and part will result from actual sales (ordering materials, etc.). Thus, the higher the level of sales, the higher the telephone bill – but it is not proportional. A doubling of sales may result in the bill increasing by, say, only 30 per cent.

Staff costs are obvious – or are they? Some of the staff will be involved in providing the service or making the goods but others will be doing work which, while essential, is not directly related to production. That makes matters a bit more complex (and explains why the way in which the staff costs are shown in the final accounts can vary – it is to reflect some of the complications). However, when costing a business all that matters is that the total cost of staff is known.

In order to see how costing works in practice, we will consider a few examples.

A Market Stall
This is probably one of the simplest of all cases. What is involved? The stallholder must buy his goods, get them to the market and set up his stall. We will use a leatherwork stall run by Bill in this example.

Direct Costs:	The cost of the goods Bill buys.
Staff Costs:	None.
Fixed Costs:	The rentals paid to the market providers. The cost of insuring the stock. The basic cost of providing the vehicle (e.g. tax and insurance).
Overhead Costs:	The telephone bill (used to source goods, etc.). Travelling costs to fetch goods. Travelling costs to markets. Stationery – minimum an accounts book. Postage. Bank Charges. Professional Fees – e.g. the Accountant.

Now let us put some figures in place and see what happens. It is not the figures that matter, just the principles. All the figures used throughout this book are given as examples only and can be invalidated by the passage of time or by changes in legislation.

Bill decides he will attend four markets each week so that he has time to collect and sort out his stock.

The first problem he faces is to decide exactly what sort of leather goods will sell and what level of sales can be expected. Having looked at various markets, talked to a number of stallholders and contacted several suppliers, he decides to stock handmade handbags and belts although, of course in practice, he would carry a far wider range of goods than in this example.

He finds he can buy the sort of bags he wants for an average of £22 each and belts for an average of £9. He checks in the shops in the towns where he plans to go and they sell similar bags at £40 and similar belts at £16 – in other words at about 180 per cent of cost. Clearly he has to be able to undercut those prices if he is to make any significant sales and he determines that, if he can sell at 80 per cent of the shop prices, he should be able to sell on average 8 bags and 15 belts per market.

The second job is to work out whether or not those sales offer him sufficient profit. Note that we want annual figures. Thus £32 (price he will charge for the bags) × 8 (number sold per day) × 4 (markets per week) × 52 (weeks) = £53,248. Belts are calculated the same way. Thus £12 (price he will charge) × 15 (number sold per day) × 4 × 52 = £37,440. Although in all calculations related to projections many of the figures used will be estimates – or even intelligent guesses – all calculations should be carried out properly. If you take estimates and then approximate the calculations it is possible to end up with a complete nonsense. The calculation is as follows:

Sales	Bags	53,248
	Belts	37,440
		90,688
Direct Costs	Bags	36,608
	Belts	28,080
		64,688

The direct cost calculations are the same as for sales, but using the cost price instead of the selling price.

Gross Profit = Sales MINUS Direct Costs = £26,000

Fixed Costs	Market Rents £100/Week	5,200
	Stock Insurance	550
	Vehicle Tax and Insurance	540
		6,290

These figures should be accurate. It does not take that long to check how much the market rentals will be or to obtain quotations for insurance whilst motor tax is a fixed amount. However, having said that, the position regarding insurance has changed considerably since this book was first written. By no means all insurance companies will consider covering market traders – with the result that not all market traders now carry proper insurance. However, help is at hand. Each local authority with markets within its control will have an officer, usually called the Market Inspector, who is responsible for the safe and proper operation of markets. In addition, the authority may well run a Market Traders' Association. Either way, they should be able to suggest insurance companies or brokers who can assist.

Profit after Fixed Costs = Gross Profit MINUS Fixed Costs = £19,710

Overhead Costs	Telephone	925
	Travelling Costs	3,250
	Stationery	300
	Postage	300
	Bank Charges	500
	Accountant	520
		5,795

At this stage, overhead costs cannot be more than reasonably accurate estimates and so they should err on the high side, as we saw above.

Net Profit before Tax = Sales MINUS all costs = £13,915

This makes the broad assumption that the estimated sales will be achieved. Bill decides he will carry out a 'sensitivity test' on the basis that he actually makes less than predicted sales.

That is done as follows – remember that the Predicted Gross Profit is £26,000:

PGP reduced by	50%	40%	30%	20%	10%
PGP reduced to	13,000	15,600	18,200	20,800	23,400
LESS Fixed Costs	6,290	6,290	6,290	6,290	6,290
	6,710	9,310	11,910	14,510	17,110
LESS Overheads	5,795	5,795	5,795	5,795	5,795
Reduced Net Profit	915	3,515	6,115	8,715	11,315

Even in this simple example, we see the advantages of dividing the costs up. Instead of having to go right back to sales, we can start with the gross profit because that is directly proportional to the turnover. Note that it is assumed that overhead costs will not vary – usually they do but in a sensitivity test they can be left at the higher figure quite safely as the variation will be down, not up.

Whether or not Bill goes ahead with this business will depend on two factors: the minimum amount he needs in order to live and the level of sales that he is *absolutely certain he can achieve*. He probably had a bit of a shock when he carried out the sensitivity exercise and looked at the bottom line. He may even have felt that he really did need to rethink his plans before taking the plunge.

Before we leave Bill to take his decision, there is some advantage in looking at the figures we produced in terms of percentage of sales, thus:

Sales	90,688	100%
Direct Costs	64,688	72%
Gross Profit	**26,000**	**28%**
Fixed Costs	6,290	7%
Overhead Costs	5,795	7%
Net Profit	**13,915**	**15%**

Note these figures are rounded to the nearest whole number – up in the case of costs and down in the case of profits. This is why the figures don't quite add up. 72 + 28 = 100 but 7 + 7 + 15 = 29 and not 28.

The reason for producing these figures is twofold. Later, when the business has been running for a while, Bill – if he is sensible – will want to make sure that the business is 'on target'. It is far easier to compare percentages rather than figures, apart from, of course, the turnover figure where actual has to be compared against projected.

The most important of those is the gross profit – in this case 28 per cent – although, in this example it is not likely to vary. We shall return to this when we look at more complicated examples.

You will remember that Bill decided on the average sales that he could expect when he was working out his turnover. It would be wrong to think that these will be made on a regular basis. For example, he will certainly sell more per market just before Christmas and, if any of his markets are in tourist areas, he will generally be busier during the holiday season.

This can be important. If he proposes to start in the late autumn or early summer, he will benefit from these increased sales early in the life of his new business – but must beware the leaner times to come. If he starts at the end of one of these peak periods, he will have to be able to survive some weeks of lower takings – and must ensure that he has enough to live on to see him through that time.

This raises the question of the best time to start a business. Obviously it varies but in this case there are a couple of arguments that Bill might care to consider. If he is working in an area where holidaymakers will make little difference, his most important 'peak' will be Christmas. It is possible that starting in early autumn, so that those who visit the market regularly are aware of his stall before they start their Christmas shopping, could well lift his takings in that critical period. Obviously, the worst time to start would be in January. However, if holidaymakers are important, he might consider starting at the beginning of the holiday season. There is no point in creating 'customer awareness' as each batch of holiday-makers will be encountering him for the first time.

A General Trade

This sort of calculation applies in any situation where the customer will be supplied with labour and materials. The hourly rate that can be charged will depend on the general charges made in the locality.

A very good rule is that the labour charges should provide as a minimum the amount needed to meet all the costs of the business plus a minimum profit. Then any profit made on the supply of materials is a bonus. The reason for adopting this approach is that it is conceivable (if not probable) that the tradesman will pick up a run of business where all materials are supplied.

In this case, we shall be working in a different order as follows:

Fixed Costs	Workshop Rent	3,600
	General Insurance	740
	Vehicle Tax and Insurance	540
		4,880

These figures are similar to the market trader's except for insurance which will be higher as it has to include liability cover.

Overhead	Telephone	920
Costs	Travelling Costs	3,750
	Stationery	350
	Postage	350
	Bank Charges	575
	Accountant	600
		6,454

Now, if the minimum that we need to earn is £15,000 we add these three figures together. 15,000 + 4,880 + 6,454 = £26,334. Our *minimum* hourly rate is that divided by the number of actual hours work we can charge out in 12 months. For a start, we shall need time to collect materials, drive to the work place, look at work in order to provide estimates and a good deal of general running about – none of which can be charged to a customer. If we manage to achieve 30 hours charged work a week, we shall be doing quite well. Based on, say, 48 working weeks (two weeks holiday plus various bank holidays and an allowance for a few days' sickness) that means we can charge for 1,440 hours per annum. 26,334 divided by 1,440 is £18.2875 – call it £18.

The question we have to ask is quite simple. Is this a reasonable rate for this trade in this area? You may well find that the rate charged locally in the trade you are considering is nearer £15 per hour – which is why so many tradesmen working on their own offer some sort of specialty which moves them from this category to a specialist trade.

A Specialist Trade
This I define as a trade which provides a particular service which guarantees that profits will be made on materials as well as labour.

A simple example is the plumber who specialises in installing central heating systems. He can calculate the average cost of the materials used for every hour of labour. Let us say that that figure is £20. In other words, the cost of buying the materials to install a central heating system, which will take 30 hours of labour, is £600.

As a tradesman you are getting a 15 per cent discount on those materials, so the minimum oncost you should add is 15 per cent, although 25 per cent would not be too much. At 25 per cent (remember, that is 25 per cent of the sales price to the customer, not 25 per cent of the cost price) that £20 becomes 20/75 × 100 or £26.67. That means that you will be making just over £6 profit every working hour from the materials that you supply. If you want to make £18 per hour, your hourly labour rate can be dropped by that £6 to become £12, which may well give you a price advantage over your competitors. However, jobs of this type are usually against estimate rather than on an hourly basis which means that you can charge whatever the market will bear – so long as you achieve the minimum hourly rate of £18 including material oncosts.

Again, the final decision is based on whether or not, having fixed the prices, you believe that there is a large enough demand to enable you to sell 30 hours of your time at that price each week.

A Café
This example will enable us to look at some of the complications that arise – and see how to deal with them.

Jane, having decided to open a small tea room, has been looking for a shop she can rent which has the appropriate planning permissions. Apart from planning permissions she will have to make sure that the establishment complies with the requirements of the Health & Safety Executive. She finds just what she wants, a small shop previously used as a restaurant on the edge of the prime shopping and commercial area but also close to the point where summer visitors tend to congregate.

The shop area will take twelve tables: eight to seat four persons and four to seat two. In technical terms that means she can serve 40 covers.

She decides that she will open for morning coffees, lunches and afternoon teas. This is mainly because the town is well-served by places offering evening meals but she has determined that there is room for a further café during the day.

At best, she can expect to serve no more than 30 covers for coffees at one time – a café looks full when all the tables are occupied even when some of those that will seat four are being used by two people. If the morning session lasts two hours and each person stays for an average of thirty minutes, she could serve 120 covers per session. However, she decides to be cautious and to base her calculations on 60 covers in the winter and 80 in the summer.

The same will apply when considering afternoon teas.

Lunchtimes will be different. As it is a busy, commercial town there is the possibility that she could reach maximum numbers twice each day – i.e. 80 covers per session.

This sort of establishment succeeds because it offers customers what they want at the right price in the right atmosphere with the right service. It is usual, therefore, to start by designing the menus. Jane settles on the following (these prices are, of course, given for illustrative purposes only, and are in no sense suggestions):

General Menu served 10 am to 6.30 pm

Coffee: £1.00 per cup or £1.20 per mug
Tea: 85p per single person pot
Hot Chocolate: £1.10 per cup or £1.30 per mug
Biscuits (selection of six): £1.00
Buttered Toast: 30p per round
Toasted Teacakes: 50p each
Sandwiches – Beef, Ham or Cheese: £1.10
Sandwiches – Toasted: £1.40

Luncheon Menu served 12 noon to 2 pm

Soup of the Day: £1.40
(served with roll and butter)
Hot Pot of the Day: £2.20
Ham, Eggs and Chips: £2.50
Homemade Steak and Kidney Pie: £2.60
(served with peas and chips)
Selection of Puddings: £1.40

Afternoon Menu served from 2 pm to 6.30 pm

Cream Teas: £2.60
(Scones, Jam, Clotted Cream and Pot of Tea)
Selection of Cakes: £1.00

Obviously the menu would not be exactly as shown but the above enables us to explore the points we need to consider. It is important to note that the prices will reflect not just the quality of the food but the sort of service offered. If waiting staff are to be employed, the prices will be higher than in a self-service establishment. In this case, Jane will be using waiters and waitresses.

Sales
This time, life is infinitely more complex than it was with the previous examples. We will explore it in detail so that the mechanisms used in even the most complicated businesses can

be demonstrated. Although most people would not go to this amount of trouble for the sort of café we have in mind, this is exactly how I proceed when assisting a client considering starting up almost any business. This is because it is as accurate as possible and, even more important, it creates a 'chart' against which the business progress can be compared in the early years.

We need to produce a 'spreadsheet'. All my spreadsheets are produced on a computer but a suitably ruled piece of paper, a pencil, a calculator and a rubber are all that you need – it just takes longer, much longer!

Now, the day is split into three sessions as far as Jane is concerned: morning, lunchtime and afternoon. Overlaying that division is the fact that weekdays will be different from Saturdays and Sundays which will be different from each other. Add to that the fact that this is a seasonal operation and the need for some type of spreadsheet becomes obvious.

Spreadsheet 1 looks complicated but is, in fact, quite simple when you take it to pieces.

We will assume that Jane intends to start the business in April. The first job is to leave a column for titles and then head each of the next twelve columns with the month – starting with the first month.

Now, we know that weekdays will be different from Saturdays or Sundays so we need to know how many of each will fall in each month. We start by putting in the titles in the left-hand column beginning with 'Weekdays in month', leaving a few lines for our subsequent calculations and repeat this for both Saturdays and Sundays. Now we count the number in each month and enter that number under the appropriate month for each of our three sections.

Morning Coffees: It is logical to start with weekdays. Jane has determined that the maximum number of covers she could serve during the morning sessions is 60 during the winter and 80 during the summer.

Before she can go any further she has to decide just what she means by 'winter' and 'summer'. After looking at some of the brochures for hotels in her area, she discovers that most of those that stay open all the year split the year into four: June to

SPREADSHEET 1 Initial Sales and Gross Profit Calculations

	Apr	May	Jun	Jul	Aug	Sep	Oct	Nov	Dec	Jan	Feb	Mar	Totals
Weekdays in Month	21	22	22	21	23	22	21	22	22	21	20	23	
Morning Coffees/day	60	70	80	80	80	70	60	60	60	60	60	60	
Estimated Spend/cover	1.60	1.60	1.60	1.60	1.60	1.60	1.60	1.60	1.60	1.60	1.60	1.60	
Estimated Sales	2,016.00	2,464.00	2,816.00	2,688.00	2,944.00	2,464.00	2,016.00	2,112.00	2,112.00	2,016.00	1,920.00	2,208.00	27,776.00
Lunches/day	60	70	80	80	80	70	60	60	60	60	60	60	
Estimated Spend/cover	4.30	4.30	4.30	4.30	4.30	4.30	4.30	4.30	4.30	4.30	4.30	4.30	
Estimated Sales	5,418.00	6,622.00	7,568.00	7,224.00	7,912.00	6,622.00	5,418.00	5,676.00	5,676.00	5,418.00	5,160.00	5,934.00	74,648.00
Afternoon Teas/day	60	70	80	80	80	70	60	60	60	60	60	60	
Estimated Spend/cover	1.80	1.80	1.80	1.80	1.80	1.80	1.80	1.80	1.80	1.80	1.80	1.80	
Estimated Sales	2,268.00	2,772.00	3,168.00	3,024.00	3,312.00	2,772.00	2,268.00	2,376.00	2,376.00	2,268.00	2,160.00	2,484.00	31,248.00
Saturdays in Month	5	4	4	5	4	4	5	4	5	5	4	4	
Morning Coffees/day	60	70	80	80	80	70	60	60	60	60	60	60	
Estimated Spend/cover	1.60	1.60	1.60	1.60	1.60	1.60	1.60	1.60	1.60	1.60	1.60	1.60	
Estimated Sales	480.00	448.00	512.00	640.00	512.00	448.00	480.00	384.00	480.00	480.00	384.00	384.00	5,632.00
Lunches/day	60	70	80	80	80	70	60	60	60	60	60	60	
Estimated Spend/cover	3.50	3.50	3.50	3.50	3.50	3.50	3.50	3.50	3.50	3.50	3.50	3.50	
Estimated Sales	1,050.00	980.00	1,120.00	1,400.00	1,120.00	980.00	1,050.00	840.00	1,050.00	1,050.00	840.00	840.00	12,320.00
Afternoon Teas/day			80	80	80								
Estimated Spend/cover			1.80	1.80	1.80								
Estimated Sales			576.00	720.00	576.00								1,872.00
Sundays in Month		5	4	5	4	4							
Morning Coffees/day		42	48	48	48	42							
Estimated Spend/cover		1.60	1.60	1.60	1.60	1.60							
Estimated Sales		336.00	307.20	384.00	307.20	268.80							1,603.20
Lunches/day		70	80	80	80	70							
Estimated Spend/cover		2.50	2.50	2.50	2.50	2.50							
Estimated Sales		875.00	800.00	1,000.00	800.00	700.00							4,175.00
Afternoon Teas/day			80	80	80								
Estimated Spend/cover			1.80	1.80	1.80								
Estimated Sales			576.00	720.00	576.00								1,872.00
Total Estimated Sales	11,232.00	14,497.00	17,443.20	17,800.00	18,059.20	14,254.80	11,232.00	11,388.00	11,694.00	11,232.00	10,464.00	11,850.00	161,146.20
LESS 25%	2,808.00	3,624.25	4,360.80	4,450.00	4,514.80	3,563.70	2,808.00	2,847.00	2,923.50	2,808.00	2,616.00	2,962.50	40,286.55
Predicted Annual Sales	8,424.00	10,872.75	13,082.40	13,350.00	13,544.40	10,691.00	8,424.00	8,541.00	8,770.50	8,424.00	7,848.00	8,887.50	120,859.65
LESS Direct Costs @ 35%	2,948.40	3,805.46	4,578.84	4,672.50	4,740.54	3,741.89	2,948.40	2,989.35	3,069.68	2,948.40	2,746.80	3,110.63	42,300.88
Predicted GROSS PROFIT	5,475.60	7,067.29	8,503.56	8,677.50	8,803.86	6,949.22	5,475.60	5,551.65	5,700.83	5,475.60	5,101.20	5,776.88*	78,558.77

August (Summer or High Season); September; October to April (Winter or Low Season); May. September and May are referred to as the 'Shoulder Seasons' and Jane decides that the maximum covers during those months will be 70.

Next she needs to estimate the average spend per head during the morning sessions. Almost all customers will have a beverage (say 95p on average) and she estimates that 50 per cent will have something else (say £1.30 on average, which equals 65p per cover). Thus she expects morning coffee sales to average £1.60 per head – and the month by month value of those sales is calculated by multiplying £1.60 by the number expected each day and the number of days in the month.

Jane believes that Saturday mornings, when there will be fewer business people around but more shoppers, will be similar to weekdays but that Sunday mornings will be different. For a start, Jane intends to be open on Sundays, only from May to September. She does not expect Sunday morning sessions to generate more than 60 per cent of the weekday covers, regardless of season.

Lunchtimes: The average spend at lunchtime will be far higher. Some will have a starter, main course and pudding; some a starter and pudding; some a main course and pudding. The combinations are numerous. However, working on a 'worst case' basis, Jane set this figure at £4.30.

After some thought, Jane decides that the average spend at the weekends will be slightly lower and opts for £3.50 (roughly 80 per cent) for Saturdays and £2.50 (roughly 60 per cent) for Sundays.

Afternoon Teas: During the summer season, cream teas are likely to prove very popular and could well account for about half of all afternoon sales. The other half would be made up of people calling in for tea, coffee or a soft drink. This would result in an average summer spend of £1.30 (50 per cent of the sales price of a cream tea) plus – say – 50p (50 per cent of the sales price of a cup of coffee) or £1.80. She decides there would be no point in offering afternoon teas at the weekends, except during the summer, and that there is no reason to believe that the weekends would be very different from weekdays.

Add together the sales from each section for each month and we find that the Total Estimated Sales figure is £161,146. Obviously a good deal of guesswork has been used to arrive at these figures. However, every single 'guess' has been based on logic and is the best that we can do at this stage.

However, few cafés operate at 100 per cent of potential – even when they are established (and we will be looking at the build up to the established turnover in the next chapter). Jane, following an attack of nervousness, decides she will base her calculations on achieving 75 per cent of her prediction. Accordingly, all sales figures are multiplied by 0.75 to give us a final figure of £120,860 which is her *Predicted Annual Sales* for the first year.

Direct Costs

As we have already seen, when someone has a good working knowledge of a business, he or she can work in terms of average percentages when calculating gross profit from sales. The average percentage on a trade by trade basis can be taken from the statistics kept by most banks or from an accountant who handles that particular trade.

Better still, Jane could cost out every dish and arrive at a calculated direct cost percentage. That is really the right way to tackle the job but it does mean actually buying and preparing every dish in order to arrive at an accurate figure as, in this business, wastage will have to be taken into consideration. Jane decides to do this and, at the end of exhaustive (and exhausting) trials, Jane discovers that it will probably cost her 35 per cent of sales in direct costs. She can now calculate her predicted gross profit as shown on the spreadsheet to arrive at a predicted gross profit of £78,559.

Staff Costs

First decision: how many people are required? The café will be open from 10 am to 6.30 pm. Allowing three quarters of an hour at each end of the day for 'housekeeping' that means staff cover for 10 hours each day (Sundays, when open, 8 hours).

One cook should be sufficient. He (or she) would need to start at about 9.40 am and finish at 2.30 pm Mondays to Saturdays in the winter, making a standard 35 hour week.

One kitchen assistant and one waiter/waitress would be needed from 9.15 am to 7.15 pm (2.45 pm on Saturdays in the winter) and probably an additional kitchen assistant and waiter/waitress from 11.45 am to 2.45 pm. Obviously this can be achieved only using some form of split shift system. For the basic week as worked in the winter season, two kitchen assistants and two waiters/waitresses each working 36.75 hours meets this requirement.

In the summer, either further part-time staff would be needed or permanent staff would need to work overtime.

We can now start to calculate the costs.

Post	Hrs/Week	Hrs/Annum	Rate	Annual Cost
Cook	35.0	1,820	6.00	10,920
Kitchen Assistants	73.5	3,822	4.10	15,670
Waiting staff	73.5	3,822	4.10	15,670
				42,260

During the 20 weeks of the shoulder and summer season, additional hours are needed. Whether these are carried out by staff working overtime or casual labour, it is sensible to cost them at time and a half. These additional costs are:

Post	Hrs/Week	Hrs/Annum	Rate	Annual Cost
Cook	5.0	100	9.00	900
Kitchen Assistants	15.0	300	6.15	1,845
Waiting staff	15.0	300	6.15	1,845
				4,590

Thus we have a total predicted staff cost of £46,850 but we must remember that we shall be paying National Insurance contributions. A good rule of thumb is to add 11 per cent to cover these and other staff oriented costs. Thus we arrive at a final figure of £52,004.

Legal Minimum Wage
One of the problems associated with running a small business
– and one that is especially true when considering a small tea
room or café – is the impact on the wage costs of legislation
which determines a minimum wage.

This legislation has been changed since it was first
introduced and is likely to change again. It follows that it is
most important to check the law in this regard when you
first consider employing other people. At the moment those
who employ only a small workforce are exempt from the
regulations as are employees below a certain age – but both
are likely to change which is why no figures are quoted
here.

Fixed Costs
As we have seen, these are determined by obtaining the facts.

Fixed Costs	Rent	4,850
	Business Rates	1,940
	General Insurance	875
	Vehicle Tax and Insurance	500
		8,165

Overhead Costs
These are estimated.

Overhead Costs	Telephone	460
	Travelling Costs	700
	Stationery	575
	Postage	184
	Repairs and Renewals	575
	Advertising	600
	Sundries	525
	Bank Charges	575
	Accountant	980
		5,174

Projected Profit and Loss Account

Gross Profit	78,559
LESS Staff Costs	52,004
LESS Fixed Costs	8,165
LESS Overhead Costs	5,174
	13,216

This is a little less than Jane had hoped but she decides to proceed on the basis that she can manage on that profit. In any event, all her sales predictions have been pessimistic and she feels it reasonable to hope that she will improve on them.

Finally
The above examples offer the basics behind costing almost all small businesses as all the elements have been covered. Many businesses operate with more than one 'profit centre' and the way in which each is handled may vary. Thus a garage facility with workshops, forecourt, shop and car showroom has at least four profit centres (five if there is an MOT bay) each of which is a little different. The steps we take are as follows:

1. Calculate predicted sales for each profit centre.
2. Calculate predicted direct costs for each profit centre.
3. Calculate total predicted gross profit.
4. Calculate staff costs.
5. Determine fixed costs.
6. Estimate overhead costs.
7. Calculate predicted net profit.

Because each step is fairly simple (and we can make sure we keep it simple by producing a spreadsheet for each profit centre), we can deal with a highly complex situation without too much difficulty.

5

SETTING UP COSTS

In the last chapter we looked at ensuring that the business, once running, would provide us with the profits that we want to make. The next job is to calculate the amount of cash we need to find in order to take the business from scratch to optimum profitability.

In some ways this should have been Chapter 4 and vice versa because one of the running costs that we ignored was the cost of borrowing money and we shall not know how much (if any) we are going to need to borrow (and thus what it will cost) until we have carried out the work described below. But, just to complicate matters, we cannot complete the calculations which follow without first establishing the profit profile. It is, in fact, a chicken and egg situation which is most easily solved using a computer with a spreadsheet program, although it can be done with pencil and paper (and rubber).

We will make a start by looking further at Jane's proposal.

Ingoings
Since Jane will be renting the shop we can ignore the costs associated with buying the property in which the business will be housed, at least for the time being. However, there are a number of costs which she will have to bear associated with moving into the property and these are all lumped together under this heading.

Various people specify Ingoings differently – for our purposes the best definition is 'any cost which will not be repeated and which will not provide us with a tangible asset' (i.e. excluding furniture, plant, equipment, stock, etc.).

The first which will nearly always apply is the cost of taking legal advice before signing any leases – the Legal Fees. Unless you know a good deal about the laws of contract, it is usually sensible to have any contract (and that includes a lease) checked out by your solicitor.

There may or may not be the need for a premium. This is a charge made by the landlord for granting the lease and the usual rule is that a lease with a high premium calls for fairly low rents and vice versa.

The property may need to be refurbished before it can be occupied. This covers everything from a quick coat of paint to fairly major building works.

Jane's Ingoings
Jane, sensibly, approached a number of solicitors and asked them to quote for checking her lease. She was surprised at the variations in these quotes and settled for one who wanted £400. This was the second lowest but she had heard bad reports of the man who quoted less and, when she visited him, frankly did not like him. She decided, rightly, that there might be times when she would need other legal advice and that she was actually selecting the solicitor who would act for the business on an ongoing basis and that she had to feel comfortable with him.

In this case the premium was small: £575 (probably set to cover the landlord's costs in granting the lease).

Because the property had been used as a restaurant, most of the basic requirements were installed. Some were not quite to Jane's liking but she felt they would do. However, the decorations and the lighting were suited to an evening operation and were far too dark and dismal for a daytime café. She obtained estimates to put these faults right and concluded that she should allow £2,750 to be on the safe side.

Thus the total ingoings amount to £3,725.

Fixtures and Fittings, Plant and Equipment
Under this heading fall all the various bits and pieces that are needed to run the operation. Whether an item is a fixture or a

fitting or a piece of plant or equipment really makes no difference to the calculations. (There may be legal complications such as the fact that, under some leases, any 'fixtures' become the landlord's property but these need not concern us at this stage.)

A complete inventory of absolutely everything needed has to be prepared and costed. Not everything needs to be new: not everything needs to be bought (although if rented or leased these costs have to be transferred back to the profit and loss calculations).

Jane's Fixtures and Fittings, Plant and Equipment
The exact details do not matter but the list covered everything from cookers to salt cellars and from refrigerators to teaspoons. Having prepared the list, Jane contacted all her local suppliers and obtained prices. She then looked round at possible secondhand sources, checking to find out whether or not any restaurant, hotel or café was closing down. In the end, she opted for some new and some secondhand but she decided that she had enough cash behind her to be able to buy everything and that the final bill for these items was going to be £9,500.

Stock
Almost every business needs some starting stock – stock that will be replaced as it is used. If a formal stock control is used, against each item there will be a 'Minimum' and 'Maximum' quantity and stock will be re-ordered when it reaches the first figure to bring it up to the second. Few small businesses are as formal with stock control as all that. It is good discipline because it avoids the two dangers: running out of something vital and carrying idle stock. Idle stock means that cash is needlessly tied up which can be critical in the early months of any business.

In Jane's case, there will be a need for certain items to be bought virtually daily if she intends to use fresh ingredients. Those can be ignored when considering initial stock. Even if you are not going to run a 'minimax' control system, at this stage you should prepare a list of all items required, determine prices, consider which items would move fast enough to make it worthwhile going for a larger quantity if there are quantity discounts available and decide on how much of each you will need to start with. Last of all, decide when you need that stock available.

Jane's Stock
Jane carried out the above exercise and found that there was a good deal of her stock requirements that could be obtained through a local cash-and-carry at prices which compared favourably with goods delivered by wholesalers whose price advantages only applied with orders far larger than Jane was considering. She decided that the advantages of using the cash-and-carry (good prices and quick access which meant carrying lower levels of stock) outweighed the disadvantages (cost of petrol and time) and so selected a fairly low level of starting stock which she costed at £1,750.

Since the first month was going to be taken up by the electricians and decorators, this would not be needed until month 2.

Early Trading
The above may take a good deal of time and effort if it is to be carried out properly but there is nothing particularly complicated about it. Determining the way in which the trade will build up from nothing to the predicted figures used before is a rather different matter.

Most people decide to apply a percentage to each month's predicted gross profit starting low and gradually building up to 100 per cent. To be honest, whilst it is probably as good a way as any, it is extremely unlikely to reflect reality.

Jane's Early Trading
Like most people, Jane really has no idea how quickly the business will build up. She decides to follow a prediction which she judges is 'playing safe': no sales in month 1 (because of the refurbishment) and then a build up as shown on Spreadsheet 2. (Note the comment about the tourist trade.) This is actually a very fast build up and she would have been

wiser to have spread it over a full twelve months. However, in this chapter I am not really concerned with the figures I am using so much as the way in which they are handled.

Bringing it all Together

Spreadsheet 2 brings all the figures together in a consolidated cash flow for the first year and *Spreadsheet 3* looks at the second year. Always cover all years affected by the build-up period plus one at 100 per cent prediction.

We have not bothered to bring forward all the figures from Spreadsheet 1 as these are not needed. We start with the predicted gross profit and then apply the build-up factor. We include all the other costs: ingoings, staff, fixed costs and overheads.

It should be noted that we have not allocated the overheads quite as accurately as we could have done. We have arrived at a monthly figure by dividing the total amount by 12. A higher degree of accuracy can be achieved by estimating overheads on a monthly basis so that quarterly accounts, such as the telephone bill, are in the right months. However, in this case the resulting error will be quite small and can be safely ignored.

The other point to notice is that Jane's personal drawings are included. It may sound odd, but when people work out this sort of spreadsheet, they often completely forget that the whole purpose of the business is to provide them with an income. However, don't overdo it – put down what you need and no more. The time for luxuries is when the business is making profits.

Conclusions

The most important line on this Spreadsheet is the 'Running Net Surplus' line which shows the amount of money that is needed to start the business. In this case the peak requirement is in the eleventh month and is £29,515. This is the amount of cash that Jane needs to have available to start the business. Secondly, we can see that the business should provide a cash surplus of nearly £6,400 from year two. Since the deficit carried forward from that year is £23,010 it will take nearly

SPREADSHEET 2 Predicted Trading Account for Year One

	Apr	May	Jun	Jul	Aug	Sep	Oct	Nov	Dec	Jan	Feb	Mar	Totals
Predicted Gross Profit	5,475.60	7,067.29	8,503.56	8,677.50	8,803.86	6,949.22	5,475.60	5,551.65	5,700.83	5,475.60	5,101.20	5,776.88	78,558.77
Adjustment for year 1 trading	0%	30%	60%	90%	90%	50%	60%	70%	80%	90%	100%	100%	
CASH INFLOW	0.00	2,120.19	5,102.14	7,809.75	7,923.47	3,474.61	3,285.36	3,886.16	4,560.66	4,928.04	5,101.20	5,776.88	53,968.44
CASH OUTFLOW													
Ingoings	3,725.00												3,725.00
Fixtures, Fittings, etc	9,500.00												9,500.00
Initial Stock		1,750.00											1,750.00
Personal Drawings	575.00	575.00	575.00	575.00	575.00	575.00	575.00	575.00	575.00	575.00	575.00	575.00	6,900.00
Staff Costs	4,928.08	4,928.08	4,928.08	4,928.08	4,928.08	4,928.08	3,909.08	3,909.08	3,909.08	3,909.08	3,909.08	3,909.08	48,094.92
Fixed Costs	680.00	680.00	680.00	680.00	680.00	680.00	680.00	680.00	680.00	680.00	680.00	680.00	8,160.00
Overhead Costs	431.00	431.00	431.00	431.00	431.00	431.00	431.00	431.00	431.00	431.00	431.00	431.00	5,172.00
Total Cash Outflow	14,911.00	8,364.08	6,614.08	6,614.08	6,614.08	6,614.08	5,595.08	5,595.08	5,595.08	5,595.08	5,595.08	5,595.08	83,301.92
Net Surplus	(14,911.00)	(6,243.90)	(1,511.95)	1,195.67	1,309.39	(3,139.48)	(2,309.72)	(1,708.93)	(1,034.42)	(667.04)	(493.88)	181.79	
Running Net Surplus	(14,911.00)	(21,154.90)	(22,666.84)	(21,471.18)	(20,161.79)	(23,301.26)	(25,610.99)	(27,319.91)	(28,354.34)	(29,021.38)	(29,515.26)	(29,333.47)	

NOTE: The business will not progress in a steady fashion because as far as the tourists are concerned this is not a new business – hence the higher figures for June, July and August.

SPREADSHEET 3 Predicted Trading Account for Year Two

	Apr	May	Jun	Jul	Aug	Sep	Oct	Nov	Dec	Jan	Feb	Mar	Totals
CASH INFLOW													
Predicted Gross Profit	5,475.60	7,067.29	8,503.56	8,677.50	8,803.86	6,949.22	5,475.60	5,551.65	5,700.83	5,475.60	5,101.20	5,776.88	78,558.77
CASH OUTFLOW													
Personal Drawings	575.00	575.00	575.00	575.00	575.00	575.00	575.00	575.00	575.00	575.00	575.00	575.00	6,900.00
Staff Costs	3,909.08	4,928.08	4,928.08	4,928.08	4,928.08	4,928.08	3,909.08	3,909.08	3,909.08	3,909.08	3,909.08	3,909.08	52,004.00
Fixed Costs	680.00	680.00	680.00	680.00	680.00	680.00	680.00	680.00	680.00	680.00	680.00	680.00	8,160.00
Overhead Costs	431.00	431.00	431.00	431.00	431.00	431.00	431.00	431.00	431.00	431.00	431.00	431.00	5,172.00
Total Cash Outflow	5,595.08	6,614.08	6,614.08	6,614.08	6,614.08	6,614.08	5,595.08	5,595.08	5,595.08	5,595.08	5,595.08	5,595.08	72,236.00
Net Surplus	(119.48)	453.20	1,889.48	2,063.42	2,189.78	335.13	(119.48)	(43.43)	105.74	(119.48)	(493.88)	181.79	6,322.77
Running Net Surplus	(29,452.96)	(28,999.75)	(27,110.28)	(25,046.86)	(22,857.08)	(22,521.95)	(22,641.43)	(22,684.87)	(22,579.13)	(22,698.61)	(23,192.49)	(23,010.70)	

four years (i.e. six years in total) before the business has repaid the initial investment.

Jane may have that sort of cash, she may have some of it and need to borrow the rest or she may need to borrow all of it (and we shall be looking at commercial loans in another chapter). The cruel fact is that she *must* have that sum *available* or she is liable to run out of cash at a critical moment and be forced to close down. In this context, 'available' means either in the bank – building society or wherever – or an offer of cash backed by a cast iron promise.

It is absolutely pointless working out the cash requirement and then either ignoring it or going back and playing with the figures to try and reduce it. The first is plain stupid and the second not far behind. The figures that we used to work out Jane's cash requirement were her best estimates of the sales that she thought she could be sure to achieve and the cost estimates reflected what she felt she needed to run the business. Any change must be to move away from her best estimates onto potentially very slippery ground.

That does not mean to say that there are not areas where she can rethink the situation. She could, as an example, think in terms of a self-service operation to reduce staff costs – this would mean a reduction in menu prices so the effect would not be that dramatic. She could restrict opening hours slightly which would also lower the wages. She could look at her fittings, fixtures, plant and equipment requirements to see whether she could reduce the bill without reducing the sales potential of the operation. Any such rethink which results in a saving is acceptable – but not a revision of sales or basic costs.

Many start-ups fail before they become profitable simply because there was insufficient cash available – and often there was no attempt to calculate the amount of cash needed so that it all came as a rather horrible surprise. There are plenty of unavoidable pitfalls to snare business people without walking into one that can be predicted.

6

CORPORATE STRUCTURES

Introduction

When more than one person sets up a business there has to be some form of agreement between the people involved which covers, amongst other matters, how profits are divided, how losses are shared, how control is exercised, how cash put into the system is protected and rewarded, how capital gains are divided and who does what.

The following corporate structures are in common use and each has advantages and disadvantages. Which is chosen will depend on the business, the source of supply of the capital and the needs of the founder member or members.

The Proprietary Business

As the name suggests, this is a business owned in its entirety by one person. The person and the business are legally one and the same. If a trading title is used, the legal reality is that it is 'John Brown trading as Get Rich Quick' (you will often see 'trading as' abbreviated to t/a).

It follows that all the financial risk is taken by that one person and that all his assets (business and personal) are included in that financial risk as there is no method by which these personal assets can be divorced from the business.

On the other hand, that person can take whatever decisions he wishes without reference to anyone else (unless he is borrowing money in which case the lender may well wish to be consulted).

A second advantage is that the administrative costs of

running a proprietary business are minimal. Apart from maintaining records for HM Customs and Excise (if the business is registered for VAT) and for HM Inland Revenue (for which no formal qualifications are required) there are no other statutory requirements.

The proprietor is, of course, entitled to all the profits from the business.

Partnerships

A partnership is a business where two or more people are enjoined by an agreement to run that business jointly. This agreement may be verbal or written.

Liabilities are shared 'jointly and severally' in total and it is vital that this is understood by anyone contemplating becoming a partner in any business. It means that all the partners (jointly) are and each individual partner (severally) is responsible for *all* the partnership liabilities. Thus, a partner who has an agreed share of only 1 per cent of the business is still responsible for 100 per cent of the partnership liabilities.

The partners may have signed an agreement whereby each partner accepts the responsibility for a percentage of the liabilities. This makes no difference outside the partnership. If a partnership of two persons set up on a 50/50 basis closes down and owes, say, £100,000 and one partner cannot provide his £50,000 – in law the other partner must pay the full £100,000 to the creditor. Under the partnership agreement, the partner who paid would have a claim against the partner who failed to pay but that is an internal matter which would not be allowed to hold up payment to the creditor.

As with the proprietary business, all the personal assets of all the partners are at risk if the partnership fails.

Decisions are taken by the partners in concert – as laid down by the partnership agreement. Thus it may be that the agreement considers three partners to share in the business in the ratio of 50/30/20. Such a division would mean that every decision would require one partner (the one with the 50 per cent share) plus one other in favour to reach a positive decision whilst deadlock could be reached if the minor partners were in conflict with the major partner.

Partnership shares usually reflect the way in which the business was capitalised although other factors may be taken into consideration. For example, an expert may hold hands with a person with capital to create a business on a 50/50 basis.

From the above, it can be seen that one partner could, in the name of the partnership, take a decision which could, in an extreme example, result in not only his or her bankruptcy but also, because of the joint and several rule, the bankruptcy of his or her partners. This is why disagreements within a partnership can (and often do) lead to serious rifts between the partners which can (and often do) destroy the business. Unfortunate or stupid decisions can result in recriminations apparently out of all proportion to the offence.

If, for some reason, a partnership is the only way forward (and this is very rare), then a proper written agreement should be drawn up between the partners (and that includes married couples).

The agreement not only lays down the way in which the partnership shall be run but deals with such matters as the death or long-term disablement of a partner, the effect of a partner being found guilty of a criminal offence (especially fraud) and all the other unlikely eventualities which, nevertheless, do happen and cause considerable problems if there is no written agreement pre-determining what shall be done.

Without an agreement, there is no mechanism whereby a partner who behaves in a fashion contrary to the overall interests of the partnership can be removed from the partnership. The 'innocent' partner is then faced with a dilemma. Walk away and risk losing what is owed to him or stick it out and possibly risk far more. For this, and for other reasons, I consider a partnership agreement so important that you will find a sample agreement at the end of this chapter. If you are not prepared to have a solicitor draw up an agreement (and I strongly advise you to do that), draw up your own using the sample on page 72 as a guide. It is probably too generalised to be universally appropriate but any written agreement is better than none. Remember, any partner who contravenes the agreement has 'broken his contract' and so automatically loses all his rights under the agreement.

Administrative costs are as for a proprietary business.

Profits are shared between partners in accordance with their share in the partnership.

The Limited Liability Company

This type of company has evolved over many years to provide a framework within which businesses can operate. It follows that, for all the imperfections inherent in the system, it is the best format for all but the smallest of businesses, and the only sensible answer if capital is being introduced by people who will not be actively involved in running the business.

The concept behind the company format is that those who provide capital into the company become the shareholders in proportion to the amount of capital injected. Shareholders are rewarded by receiving dividends in proportion to their shares and are eligible to attend the Annual General Meeting to approve or otherwise the way in which the company has been run by the directors. This meeting will also determine how much of the profit (if any) shall be 'distributed' to the shareholders as dividends and how much shall be retained in the company for future use.

Voting is in accordance with the number of shares held and the meeting can replace any or all of the directors if a majority are unsatisfied with them. Indeed, the shareholders do not need to wait for the AGM to call for new directors – if a sufficient number of shareholders sign a request for an Extraordinary General Meeting, this must be held and gives the shareholders the opportunity to question and possibly replace directors at short notice.

Control of the company is in the hands of the directors who are appointed by the shareholders to manage its affairs.

In small closed companies, the chances are that the directors are also shareholders and, indeed, it may be that all shareholders are also directors.

The company is a legal entity in its own right, separate from and not really identified with the shareholders or the directors.

The term 'limited liability' leads to some confusion. When a company is created it will have an 'Authorised Shareholding' (minimum £100). That specifies the limit of the shareholders' liability and can be checked by anyone by reference to records held at Companies House. It follows that if all the shares have been issued (i.e. the shareholders have already met that liability), the shareholders are not liable for any further debts that the company may accrue.

At first sight, it would seem sensible to limit all companies to an Authorised Shareholding of £100 but that is not always possible or wise. Such a company would have great difficulty in obtaining finance other than loans secured against property unless the directors or (exceptionally) the shareholders offer 'Personal Guarantees' which removes all the protection offered by the company and exposes all the personal assets of those giving guarantees. Secured loans (Commercial Mortgages) lent against property in much the same way as a domestic mortgage are another matter.

The higher the shareholding, the stronger the company's balance sheet. An input of shareholding would show as a cash asset on one side and as further shareholding on the other. Because the shareholders are the last 'creditors' to receive cash in the event of the company being closed down, as far as the lending institutions are concerned this additional cash means that the company has additional assets against which a loan can be made.

Often, of course, a lender will not provide all the funding needed against the company assets alone and will call for directors' guarantees unless the directors and/or shareholders can borrow against personal assets in order to provide the company with the capital that it needs.

This can be done by increasing the shareholding or by making loans to the company. Those who lend in this way to companies become creditors and, should the company fail, will receive back all or a proportion of those monies, as do all other creditors.

Compare the two approaches. We will assume a small closed company with two friends who are the sole shareholders and directors.

First Approach

The bank agrees to lend the money required but insists on taking directors' guarantees. The only real wealth that the directors own is in their houses so the bank will only accept those guarantees if, in addition, it can take a charge over those houses. The company fails and the bank calls on the guarantees and, since the money is not forthcoming, takes possession of the houses. The bank will probably recoup all of the loan but the other creditors will receive little or, in extreme cases, nothing.

Second Approach
The directors decide to re-mortgage their houses to raise the cash they required. This is injected into the business by way of directors' loans. The company fails and the directors become creditors. Let us assume that creditors receive 50p in the pound. The directors receive back 50 per cent of their loans. They are left with enhanced mortgages (which may or may not be containable) but are certainly in a better position than that illustrated above.

This almost looks like a sleight-of-hand trick but is actually quite simple. In the first case, ALL the loan was 'secured' on the directors' houses and so the bank was able to take precedence over the unsecured creditors. In the second case, none of the creditors was secured (and that includes the two directors) and so the available funds were distributed in equal proportions between all those creditors. Both the outside creditors and the directors come out of it with some return because no single creditor is in a position to take all that is owed to him.

My editor has pointed out that in most cases when a limited company goes into liquidation, for the unsecured creditors to receive 50p in the pound is very unusual and 5p in the pound is nearer the going rate. He is, sadly, correct. However, why should that be so? The answer is that the directors of the company have continued trading long after it is obvious that they are going to have to close the company down. This may be because the records they have been keeping are inadequate, it may be because they are stupid or it may be because they are crooked. Working on the principle that all of my readers will be keeping proper records and that none is either stupid or crooked, I decided to stick to my 50p in the pound. In any event, the amount is not important – just the way the system works.

We have seen that the control of the company is in the hands of the directors – each of whom has an equal vote regardless of their shareholding (which may be zero). Thus, in the case we looked at before, where the capital was introduced by three people on a 50/30/20 basis, if all are directors, deadlock is impossible as any two directors can carry the decision (although at a shareholders' meeting the position would be rather different).

Administration costs are higher. Under the Companies Acts, a full return must be lodged each year and the accounts must be audited by a qualified accountant although these costs are usually quite small for smaller companies.

Once lodged, the details are available for anyone to read so become public knowledge, although smaller companies only have to lodge abbreviated information.

Directors have statutory duties which must be performed to comply with the law. These are not onerous and are intended to avoid fraud.

Directors receive a salary for work done (and are employees of the company and, as such, pay tax under Schedule E through the PAYE system).

As we have seen, shareholders receive dividends in return for providing capital.

The Combination Approach

It sometimes happens that a combination of a limited company and a proprietary business (or proprietary businesses) or of more than one limited company offers the most satisfactory structure for a given situation.

Consider someone who wishes to run a hotel and who has a friend willing to put in the starting capital required.

The friend and the main applicant form a limited liability company which buys the property and raises the required loan. The company issues 100 £1 shares, half being owned by each. The friend then holds additional shares (preferential shares) to cover the capital he injects or he makes the company a director's loan.

They then form a second limited liability company to rent and operate the hotel.

If the operation fails and the operating company is forced into liquidation, as far as the property owning company is concerned all that has happened is that it has lost its tenant. The friends can either find another tenant or form a new operating company. Either way, they have been able to protect their investment.

Generally speaking, the combination approach is only useful where the capital required is used to buy an asset which can be let to the operating entity (which need not be a limited company). In other cases, such a combination only complicates matters and offers little or no benefit.

Choosing the Right Structure

The right structure is the simplest structure that answers all requirements and the proprietary business is the simplest and should be considered first.

There are times when a proprietary business should not be used. They are:

a)   When there is more than one person involved.
b)   Where there is a high capital requirement and that capital needs to be protected.
c)   Where the business could become insolvent (as could one which buys goods and stock on credit and relies on being paid for the goods and services to settle those accounts).

In the last case, a failure by a large customer could result in the business being unable to meet its debts. Unless the business is run as a limited liability company, the owner (if a proprietary business) or owners (if a partnership) would have to make up any shortfall within the business using assets outside the business (such as a house) and would face personal bankruptcy if these assets were insufficient to meet the shortfall.

Partnerships should be considered only where there is a reasonable guarantee that the partners will not fall out – generally when they are related – but even then a written partnership agreement should be drawn up and signed (even when the partners are husband and wife).

This is because certain unusual but unfortunate events can cause serious problems if they arise. Within marriages the most common is a divorce. Probably the worst case is when one of the partners becomes mentally ill and is made a Ward of Court. Suddenly, the remaining partners find themselves in bed with a faceless bureaucracy. Between these two eventualities are many other similarly unlikely but crippling possibilities.

In my opinion, there is a far better chance of success if a limited company is set up as soon as two or more people are involved. As already mentioned, this type of corporate entity has evolved over the years. For all its faults and failings, it is the best that man has yet devised and the extra costs involved are worth it as it seems to be a framework in which people can operate most amicably.

In all fairness it should be pointed out that most accountants would disagree – but that is because their prime function is to keep costs and tax liabilities to a minimum and they are rarely involved in the absolute shambles that can follow the breakup of a partnership – a shambles in which personal relationships are often destroyed for ever.

As in so many other walks of life: you pays your money and you takes your choice.

Sample Partnership Agreement
THIS AGREEMENT is made the ... day of ... Two Thousand and ... *[use words not figures for the date]* BETWEEN ... of ... AND ... of *[enter as many names as required]*

WHEREBY IT IS AGREED that the parties hereto (hereinafter together called 'The Partners') are and become partners in the business of ... *[brief description of proposed activities]* from the ... day of ... Two Thousand and ... *[again in figures but note that the date the partnership starts may not be the date on which the agreement is signed]* upon the terms hereinafter contained namely:

1.   The firm shall be called *[trading name]*

2.   The capital of the partnership shall belong to the Partners in the proportions as to ... per cent thereof to the said ... and ... per cent thereof to the said ...

3.   The Partners shall devote their whole time and attention *[or 'such of their time and attention as may from time to time be agreed']* to the business of the partnership but shall be entitled to take an annual holiday of a duration to be agreed from time to time by the partners and shall use their best endeavours to promote the success of the partnership business

4.   The partners shall each receive each month a sum the amount to be agreed by the Partners from time to time

5.   The profits of the partnership including profits of a capital nature but excluding the drawings referred to in the previous clause shall be divided between the Partners rateably in accordance with their share of the capital as before referred to and the Partners shall bear all losses including losses of a capital nature in like proportions

6.   The usual books of account shall be kept properly

7.   The Accountant to the partnership shall be ... or such other Accountant as may from time to time be agreed by the Partners

8.   The Bankers to the partnership shall be ... or such other Bankers as may from time to time be agreed by the Partners

9.   All partnership monies not required for current expenses shall immediately upon receipt be paid into the partnership bank account

10. On the ... day of ... in each year the accounts shall be taken and a balance sheet prepared showing the assets

and liabilities of the partnership and the amount owing to each Partner in respect of capital and profits and as soon as possible thereafter the net profits (if any) shall be divided as described above

11. No Partner shall without the consent of the other Partner:

    (a) enter into any bond or become bail or surety for any person or knowingly cause or suffer to be done anything whereby the partnership property may be taken in execution or otherwise endangered

    (b) assign mortgage or charge his share in the assets or profits of the partnership

    (c) compromise or compound or (except upon payment in full) release or discharge any debts due to the partnership

    (d) contract any partnership liability or debt exceeding the sum of . . . pounds or any other such sum as may from time to time be agreed by the Partners in any one transaction

12. If either Partner shall become unable to carry out his duties pursuant to Clause 3 of this agreement for a period of not less than ten days for any reason whatsoever other than absence due to holiday Clause 11(d) of this agreement shall cease to apply until such time as the Partner is able to resume his duties. *[This clause only applies where there are only two partners. If one is just not available, 11(d) could mean that the other could not continue the business.]*

13. The partnership shall be determined by either Partner giving the other not less than six months' notice in writing *['determined' means closed down]*

14. If either Partner shall become unable to carry out his duties pursuant to Clause 3 of this agreement for a period

of not less than twenty-six weeks for any reason whatsoever then the partnership may be determined by the other Partner giving the incapacitated Partner or his personal representatives as the case may be not less than seven days' notice in writing

15. If the partnership shall be determined by notice pursuant to Clauses 13 or 14 of this agreement or dissolved by the death or bankruptcy of either Partner the Partner to whom notice is given or the surviving or solvent Partner as the case may be may within twenty-eight days of the giving of such notice or within twenty-eight days from such death or bankruptcy as the case may be by notice in writing to the other Partner or his personal representatives trustee in bankruptcy or the receiver elect as the case may be either to have the partnership wound up pursuant to the provisions of the Partnership Act 1890 or to purchase the share of the other Partner at the net value thereof as agreed between the Partner giving notice or his personal representatives trustee in bankruptcy or receiver as the case may be (hereinafter called 'The Vendor') and the other Partner (hereinafter called 'The Purchaser') or in default of such an agreement as assessed by a valuer to be nominated by the Vendor and the Purchaser jointly in writing or in default of such nomination to be appointed by . . . *[see note below about Arbitration]* and in agreeing or assessing the net value of share goodwill of the partnership shall be taken into account *[Stated simply, this clause gives the surviving partner or partners first option to purchase the share of the partner who wishes to quit, dies, becomes bankrupt or whatever. It also allows for the value of the partnership to be determined by a third party if need be.]*

16. Any valuer nominated pursuant to the last preceding clause shall act as an expert and not as an arbitrator and his professional charges shall be borne by the Vendor and the Purchaser in equal shares

17.   On the purchase by one Partner of the share of the other Partner pursuant to Clause 15 of this agreement the purchase monies shall be paid within three months from the date of determination or dissolution of the partnership and any monies outstanding after that date shall attract interest at the rate of . . . per cent per annum

18.   If the partnership shall be determined by the retirement incapacity or death of a Partner then the retiring or incapacitated Partner or the personal representatives of the deceased or incapacitated Partner as the case may be shall if so required by the other Partner continuing in the business join in an election to HM Inspector of Taxes that the business be assessed for tax purposes as a continuing business provided that the Partner continuing in the business shall indemnify the retiring or incapacitated Partner or the personal representatives of the deceased or incapacitated Partner as the case may be against any additional tax payable by such a Partner as a result of this election

19.   The Partner whose share is purchased shall not for a period of . . . years from the date of determination or dissolution directly or indirectly carry on or be concerned or interested in the business of . . . within a radius of . . . miles of any office occupied by the firm on the date of determination or dissolution alone or jointly or as director manager or employee of any other person firm or corporation

20.   Any dispute under or arising out of this agreement shall be referred in accordance with the provisions of the Arbitration Act 1950 or any statutory modification or re-enactment thereof for the time being in force to a single arbitrator to be appointed by agreement between the Partners or in default of such an agreement to be appointed by . . .

Arbitration
Clauses 15 and 20 mention the appointment of an arbitrator by a third party if agreement cannot be reached between the

partners. This raises the question as to who should make that appointment.

If the partnership runs a business which is controlled by some body (such as The Law Society or the Institute of Chartered Accountants), then it is usual to appoint 'the President for the time being of . . .' the controlling body.

If there is a relevant trade organisation (such as the Institute of Plumbers or the Electrical Contractors' Association) appoint the President of that organisation.

Another possibility is the Chairman of a Chamber of Trade or Commerce.

Note that these are all positions and not named people. The reason is that if you appoint a person you stand the risk that he or she is not available when required – he may even have died. It is, I suppose, possible that the organisation you select will no longer exist but that is a risk you will have to accept.

7

THE LIMITED COMPANY

Introduction

You need read this chapter only if you are considering a limited liability company. There are a number of ways of obtaining such a company but the easiest and cheapest is to 'buy one off the shelf'. There are firms who form companies and sell them on as their business. The advantage of buying such a company is that the basic formation procedure has been done for you and so you need have no worries on that score. The disadvantage is that you will be offered a variety of names, some of which are pretty outrageous, and you may have difficulty in finding one to your liking. However, you can always change it or adopt a trading name if that is the case.

When you buy a company you will find that there are two shares paid up – i.e. the Paid Up Capital of the firm is £2 – and that it has an authorised share capital of £100 or £1,000. Share transfer forms will come with the package to enable you to transfer those two shares to you and A N Other. If there are only two people involved, that is all that need be done at this stage as there is no real need to issue the rest of shares for the time being.

You will find that you have a Registered Number. This must appear on certain documents that the company sends out and the easiest way to ensure that you comply with this regulation is to have on all letterheads and other documents that deal with financial matters (such as invoices) the phrase 'Registered in England: Registered Number 88888888'.

Obviously if the company is registered in another country, that replaces 'England'.

The company will need a Company Secretary who is responsible for ensuring that the company fulfills all the administrative requirements called for by the various Companies Acts. Unless you have previous experience of this sort of work it probably makes sense to ask your accountant to act in this capacity. The charges for such services vary – £350 is a reasonable fee – but it is usually well worth it. The Company Secretary will advise Companies House that the company has changed hands and will provide details of the new shareholders, directors, etc. Incidentally, while you are about it you may as well ask the accountant to provide the Registered Address at his place of business. This is the address to which all official documents are sent and since these are almost invariably for the Company Secretary's attention they may as well go there in the first place. If the Registered Office is other than the usual address, letterheads, invoices, etc., must give the address of the Registered Office as well as the address for correspondence.

Financing the Company
We have already seen that the way in which a limited liability company is financed is through a combination of shareholding and debt finance. There are various forms of shareholding and it is important to understand the reasons why this should be so and the differences between them.

Ordinary Shares
As the name implies, these are the most common. The holder of an ordinary share is entitled to receive copies of the annual report and annual accounts plus the agendas and minutes of all general meetings (i.e. meetings open to the shareholders).

The shareholder is entitled to attend general meetings and to vote at them – votes being recorded by the number of shares held. If the shareholder is unable to attend the meeting but wishes to vote, he can do so by proxy or postal vote.

When all the operating costs and tax liabilities have been deducted from the company's gross sales, the cash that

remains is available for one of two purposes: to go into a
reserve account to be ploughed back into the business or to go
to the shareholders as a dividend. The directors may decide as
to which and how the division is made but are, of course,
answerable to the shareholders for that decision. Otherwise
this decision is taken by the shareholders at the Annual
General Meeting.

Thus shares attract income (called dividends) which are
linked to the profits that the company achieves.

They also have a capital value. The value of each share is
the total actual value of all the business assets less the
liabilities divided by the number of shares that have been
issued. There will also be some value attached to shares
because of the income earning potential that they possess.

It is a long and difficult job accurately to value all the
company assets. (Although the balance sheet will offer accurate figures in certain areas it is unlikely that the value of
freehold premises and certain other assets will correspond to
the 'book value' as shown in the accounts.) Furthermore, the
added income potential value is a matter of perception rather
than fact. At the end of the day, shares are really worth what
someone is prepared to pay for them. (The share values of
companies quoted on the stock exchange are based on the
price at which shares are being sold. This is why most share
prices are well above the face value of the share whilst others
may be only a fraction of that value.)

Authorised Shareholding
When a company is formed, it is 'authorised' to sell a given
number of shares – usually 100 shares each of face value £1.

For the reasons we have already seen, and in order to be
able to increase the number of shares that can be bought, this
is often increased and can become a very large number indeed.
Since stamp duty is payable on shares which are authorised,
an increase in the Authorised Shareholding involves two
costs: one to cover the administration and the other to meet the
duty. For this reason there is little point in increasing the
authorisation unless the company wishes either to borrow
money or quote for a large contract.

In both these cases the level of Authorised Shareholding will influence those making the decisions and the directors may feel that it is worth the costs involved. However, all that increasing the Authorised Shareholding does is to make a statement of intent – only when the additional shares that have been authorised are 'Paid Up' does it carry any real weight.

Paid Up Shares

These are the shares that have been issued and paid for. Although under most circumstances all the Authorised Shares will be Paid Up Shares, this is not always the case nor is it always advisable.

New companies often leave a percentage of shares to one side so that they can be sold at a later date when further finance is required, or they find there is a need to offer shares to an expert they wish to employ and, at the same time, bind more closely to the company.

Limited Liability

We have seen that the shareholders' liability is limited to the amount of the Authorised Shareholding of the company.

If all the shares have been sold, or paid up, the shareholders have fulfilled this liability and cannot be asked to provide additional funds.

If some of the shares have yet to be sold, the existing shareholders can, if the company fails, be called upon to meet the difference between the value of the Authorised Share-holding and that of the Paid Up Shareholding – a thought worth bearing in mind before increasing the authorisation.

Other Shares

Not all shares are Ordinary Shares. 'B' shares, as they are often called, are shares which are written with very different rules.

These shares are issued in order to raise funds without giving the shareholders the right to attend or vote at General Meetings.

As a result, the company will almost certainly have to offer some other incentive to potential 'B' shareholders or they will not buy the shares.

These incentives may include a guaranteed annual return and/or a guaranteed buy back agreement whereby the shares are bought back by the company at an agreed price at an agreed moment.

They may be 'preference' shares – these being shares which, in the event of the company being wound up or sold for whatever reason, will be redeemed before the ordinary shareholders receive their share. In these cases they are usually known as 'Preference Shares' rather than 'B Shares' although they are really 'B shares' with an additional benefit attached.

In some cases, the purchase of a given number of 'B shares' entitles the purchaser to buy a specified (but much smaller) number of Ordinary Shares thus giving the shareholder the same rights as the others.

Equity Participation

There are times when the company needs a loan which exceeds the amount that can be properly secured.

When this happens, some lenders will provide funding in exchange for Equity Participation. This is usually in the form of 'B shares' to cover the amount of the additional funding made plus some Ordinary Shares but may be restricted to Ordinary Shares alone. (When this is likely to happen, it is always wise to keep some of the Authorised Shares unsold and available for an Equity Partner.)

In the event of a default, this arrangement usually means that the lender takes over the business and either runs it or sells it. It follows that this type of equity partnership should be used only when all else fails.

Directors' Loans

These have been mentioned already but it is worth looking at them again and comparing them with the above ways for directors to invest in their own company.

Should a company fail, the order in which the creditors receive some return is important.

Top of the list are the secured creditors. These are the ones who have a legal charge over specified company assets. Thus the bank which lends against a mortgage over a freehold will, at the very least, receive back the amount realised when that asset is sold. If the asset sells for more than the loan, the balance is available for general distribution. HM Inland Revenue and HM Customs, as well as employees who are owed money (or who are eligible for redundancy pay), rate behind the secured creditors.

Next on the list are the unsecured creditors. These will include all the trade creditors who have supplied goods or services but whose accounts remain unpaid. It also includes those who have made unsecured loans to the company.

The fourth group are the Preference Shareholders and they are followed by the Ordinary Shareholders.

It follows that a directors' loan is in the third grouping which is why directors tend to make loans rather than take Preference Shares or increase their Ordinary Shareholding.

8

SALES

The Target Market

Once you have determined that there is a demand, you have to decide on your 'Target Market' – the people you are actually going to try to attract.

It may be that you have decided to set up a rapid document transfer courier service. (Equipment – a suitable motorcycle; skills – the ability to ride quickly but safely and to enjoy it, plus the temperament to see a job through in the specified time and a willingness to work unsocial hours.) Your market research reveals that couriers are used by a wide range of businesses but that each business is looking for a slightly different service. (For example, some seek a very rapid local document transfer during the day; others a guaranteed over-night service to other towns and cities.)

Now, do you offer a general courier service, or do you decide to find out exactly what service is needed by one type of business and concentrate on that?

In the first case, your target market is 'all local businesses'; in the second, it is 'the local solicitors' (or whatever type of business you choose). It is always tempting to think in terms of a large target market base but there are disadvantages in making it too large. If our courier goes for the solicitors, he will soon know exactly what services they want, begin to understand some of their problems and to know what price they are prepared to pay. Given that knowledge, his marketing becomes more effective. He could well end up with more work from that small target market base than he would have obtained from a larger base without the detailed knowledge of the customers' requirements.

Once you have established your target market, write down your findings. Later you will be tempted to look at other targets but any change will almost certainly be for the worse rather than the better. This is because now is the time you are really concentrating on this subject.

Marketing

Before we look at selling to the target market(s) a word or two about marketing might be helpful.

What do we mean by marketing? Usually we think of advertising and brochures and so on – what you might call the visible aspects of marketing. These are all part and parcel of the whole but represent only a small part. Marketing covers a whole range of activities designed to 'identify, anticipate and satisfy customer needs at a profit' (Chartered Institute of Marketing).

We have already looked at identifying the need but now we need to look at that need in greater detail and try to answer three more questions. They are:

When do the customers want the need fulfilled?

How do the customers want the need fulfilled?

How much are the customers prepared to pay for that fulfillment?

Having found the answers to those questions, we have to decide how best we can communicate to the target market our ability to meet their needs at a price they can afford – and communicate that ability to them at a price we can afford. There are various options we can consider and we will start with the most obvious.

Advertising

It has been said that 95 per cent of all money spent on advertising is wasted but that it takes an expert to identify which 5 per cent worked – not a cheerful thought!

Advertising takes many forms and the following is not a definitive list. However, it does cover those you are most likely to consider.

HOARDINGS AND POSTERS

This heading covers not only the large billboards but those carried on buses, railways stations and so on. Hoardings are seen repeatedly by a wide and constantly changing audience in the locality of your choice. They are usually cheap and, therefore, need to produce little in the way of sales to be cost effective. However, they have limited space and should not try to offer too much detail as many of them are seen only for moments at a time. This means they can be used only as back up publicity. There are some exceptions to that – a poster on a railway station, where people have to wait, can use quite small print and say a good deal. It is usually cheaper to buy space on a bus than on a static hoarding. Although generally just as effective, those on buses may be taken outside your chosen area and operate only when the bus is in service.

LEAFLETS

Leaflets can be distributed on a door-to-door basis (either to other businesses or to householders) or given to individuals in the street, including workers as they arrive or leave their places of work. Distributed leaflets are good for local consumer services and can be cheap to distribute (e.g. by young people). They go straight to potential customers and can carry a good deal of information. However, they can look cheap and may be discarded as 'junk mail'.

The result is that they tend to produce a low strike rate. Handing out leaflets to individuals is slightly different although the same main points apply. The basic difference is that it is possible to 'target' recipients and it can give the business a more personal feel.

Leaflets can be 'delivered' as inserts in magazines or newspapers. The former directs them to a specific audience; the latter to a specific area if local newspapers are used. Nowadays, this method is not expensive but many leaflet inserts are discarded without being read so once again the strike rate is low.

A far more effective use of leaflets, although not suited to all businesses, is to have them available in places where the target market will see them. The classic case is for businesses offering non-residential facilities to tourists and holidaymakers. Nearly all hotels, guest houses and other places offering accommodation will agree to have a supply available for their guests. If the owners consider your facility adds to the chances of people staying with them, they may well include a copy when they send out their brochure to potential guests.

The last use of the leaflet is as a small static poster on notice boards and in shop window small ad displays. These are two separate concepts. The notice board can be very effective when wishing to attract people from a group of the population who congregate together in defined places where leaflets cannot be made available. The obvious example is the use of school notice boards (if permission can be obtained) when the target market includes schoolchildren. Shop windows are different as those who spend time working through these small ads tend to be the less well-off bargain hunters. If these are a part of your target market it can be both cheap and effective. Good leaflets (or cards) stand out in these environments and time should be taken to make your leaflet as striking as possible. Incidentally, some of the superstores now have areas where you can display cards free of charge although the management reserves the right to remove any that contravene their conditions.

DIRECTORIES
These fall into two categories: local and trade.

The local directories such as Yellow Pages are a well-known source of information and advertising within them is reasonably priced. However, all similar businesses being grouped together, your entry may well be swamped by your competitors'. The problem is that it is difficult to stand out in the crowd and the temptation is to buy more and more space in an attempt to achieve. This is usually counterproductive as your competition is doing the same thing until all are spending more than can be justified by the resulting sales. The businesses that really score are those who offer a very specialist service and who end up with a heading of their own.

Some are turning to Thompsons on the basis that the cost is less and there are fewer advertisers. Unfortunately, there are also fewer readers. Even so, a cheaper advertisement in Thompsons may be more cost effective than a more expensive one in Yellow Pages.

Some communities provide local directories which are often distributed to all households in the locality. These offer fairly cheap advertising and can be cost effective. Useful for those wishing to sell to householders, their value must be questioned if your target market is other businesses or visitors.

Trade directories are different again. Although they have various advantages they are unlikely to benefit a new business as entries are expensive and often payment has to be made long before the directory is published. The nationally distributed directories are of little value to those offering local services. There are now a number of local, area and regional directories (often produced by Chambers of Trade). Some of these are available as a book or on disk for use with computers. Those who subscribe to the disk system often receive monthly or quarterly updates which overcomes the biggest objection that new businesses have to directories – the fact that they are only updated annually and it can be anything up to two years before the new business entry is published.

USING AN ADVERTISING AGENT
Whether or not an advertising agent is employed will be a matter for the individual. The decision should be based on financial reasoning. All businesses placing advertising should set an advertising budget and refuse to allow it to become overspent. It may well be that spending part of that budget with an agent proves to be more cost effective than designing your own layouts and writing your own copy even though that means you can only afford fewer or smaller advertisements.

It will depend on how good you are at designing and placing advertisements (or, more accurately, how good you think you are) and whether or not you can find a good agent. In this context, a good agent is one who has a proven track record, thoroughly understands what you are trying to do, believes in what you are trying to do and with whom you have a rapport. If you cannot find such an agent you are probably better off doing the job yourself.

TELEVISION ADVERTISING

It is highly unlikely that television advertising would apply. To launch a business using television advertising is extremely expensive – not least because of the absolute need to employ an advertising agent and production staff to generate the advertisements. Frankly, few starting up a business can contemplate the costs involved.

RADIO ADVERTISING

Radio advertising is somewhat neglected. Obviously it applies only if there are sufficient listeners from the target market(s) to make it worthwhile but it is not as expensive as one might suppose and, given the right circumstances, can be very useful. Spots of ten to thirty seconds are sold in packages of, for example, thirty slots, as radio advertising only works on repetition. Timing is very important. If teenagers are your target market, your slot must be within a programme popular with teenagers. Many business people listen to their local station as they drive to work. The main problems are the cost of production and the fact that even thirty seconds gives time for only the simplest of messages.

Even so, as I have said, radio advertising is somewhat neglected and should be considered.

MAGAZINE ADVERTISING

Magazines fall into three categories: general national, local and specialist. Although more expensive per reader than advertising in newspapers, magazine advertising is often more cost effective.

Magazines have a longer life expectancy than newspapers and are often passed on to secondary readers. Specialist magazines are read by persons with particular interests and, once the target markets have been identified, choosing the right magazine is fairly simple. However, most specialist magazines are nationals and so this usually applies only to businesses selling nationwide. Local magazines are few and far between and tend to be fairly up market.

NEWSPAPER ADVERTISING

National newspapers are widely read but expensive. They have a limited life and, although relatively cheap, are of little value to those offering local services.

Local newspaper advertising is likely to be the media most commonly used. It follows that a good working knowledge of the local press is important and, if possible, existing advertisers should be approached for their opinions. However, advertising rates are often high compared to readership and targeting is difficult.

A variation of the local newspaper is the free newspaper. Read by a large number of people and usually with low advertising rates, your advertisements may still go unnoticed as they are not read with any great care.

FEATURE ADVERTISING

Once you have started a business and that fact has become known to the advertising departments in the newspapers in your area, you will be telephoned by one of their sales staff at intervals and advised that 'We are running a special feature on ... and I am contacting you to invite you to advertise alongside the editorial.' There are only two intelligent answers: 'No, thank you' and 'I will think about it, give me 24 hours.'

It has already been mentioned that every business should set an advertising budget and stick to it. It may be that a part of that budget was allocated to 'feature advertising' in which case the second answer is the right one. If, after consideration, you feel this to be an appropriate feature, go ahead. If there is no budget allocation for this type of advertisement, the right answer is the first.

Never allow yourself to be bulldozed into taking any advertising, especially feature advertising. I have yet to meet the person who found that it paid.

STRETCHING THE ADVERTISING BUDGET

There was a time when the advertising rate card was written in tablets of stone. That is no longer the case so if you are thinking about spending a reasonable sum on advertising – regardless of the medium you have chosen – you should try haggling over the price. In most cases they will not actually agree to a reduction in the rate as such but will offer you one or two free insertions. That is a nice face-saving compromise – but you will only benefit from the competition within the advertising industry if you are prepared to bargain.

BRAD

This publication is worth mentioning. *British Rate and Data* is the definitive work which covers all advertising media in the UK. Brought out every month, it offers details of circulation, advertising rates, contacts, etc., for over 13,000 UK media opportunities, from consumer magazines to new media. Usually found in all large central libraries, it is a publication all business people who do not use an advertising agency should consult before planning any serious advertising campaign. The chances are that there will be some publication you have never heard of which offers you just what you want.

THE INTERNET

You may decide that you want to set up a web page on which to display your wares. This is a fairly complex subject (we shall be taking another look in Chapter 16) but in simple terms a web site is one that can be found by typing in an address – the web site of the publishers of this book is *www.right-way.co.uk* – or by using a 'search engine' to find what you want. Some people swear by the Internet and use it to find all the information they need; others say that making a search on it takes far too long and they would rather use conventional methods.

Media Publicity

Believe it or not, what sells newspapers and magazines is the editorial content (excluding publications for advertising only, many of which are distributed free so are not 'sold'). It follows that the editors want to know about anything you are doing that is newsworthy. The same comments apply to radio and television – especially the local stations.

If you want free publicity of this sort, you must be doing something which is newsworthy and you must make sure that the relevant media knows what you are doing.

That is a pretty glib statement; it is far harder to achieve than it sounds. However, it can be done and the way to find out how it is done is to read the appropriate papers and magazines and see what they publish and listen to your local radio station to find out what they broadcast. As a general rule, 'newsworthy' means something new – a new senior appointment, a new business starting up (even yours), a new product or service being made available, new investment into an area, new jobs being created, a new factory, shop or office being opened, etc. Apart from those, papers are looking for the unusual. As one Public Relations consultant once said: 'Tell them whenever the cat has kittens in the filing cabinet.' Remember, sending out a press release is not expensive so if they fail to print, the losses are small and if they do print, the publicity is extremely cheap.

Having said that the media sells on editorial content, it makes profits from advertising. This means that any editorial that you can give them that will attract advertising is sure to be welcome. The obvious example is the opening of a new facility which encourages the contractors and suppliers involved to advertise alongside the editorial (you will have seen this sort of thing many times).

It is worth placing the occasional advertisement with a publication that offers you this sort of publicity by way of a thank you and to encourage further such publicity even if that advertisement is unlikely to be effective. The overall impact of both editorial and advertising is used to determine cost effectiveness. I should add that all editors deny that, when they are offered a story about a business, their decision to publish or not is influenced by the advertising habits of that business. This may be true but human nature being what it is, I reserve judgment.

Direct Mail

Obviously direct mail works or we would not receive the quantities that arrive through our letterboxes almost every day.

Direct mail falls into two categories: untargeted (or blanket) and targeted.

Personally I have my doubts as to the cost effectiveness of blanket direct mail unless it can be carried out on a massive scale so that unit costs are very small – an objective probably beyond the reach of most people starting a business.

Targeted direct mail is another matter. The 'target' must be clearly defined. For a start, easily defined and obviously well worth the effort are all existing customers. We shall look at keeping customer records in a later chapter and these records are an invaluable selling aid, although this applies only where you can know who your customers are. For example, it is unlikely to apply in a shop. Whenever you bring out a new product or service, let your old customers know.

It may be that you are trying to sell to a special group (such as solicitors) in which case the creation of a direct mail list is fairly easy.

The secret with direct mail is to keep it short, keep it simple and do it often.

Word of Mouth

Meeting people and talking to them is the most effective form of selling but it is both expensive and time consuming.

Initially, the only mouths available to spread the word belong to the founders of the business. In time, representatives or agents may be employed and there will be customers to spread the word.

Incidentally, it is worth noting that the principals in any business are nearly always the best people to spread the word about a new business even if they are poor salespeople. This is because they know the business inside out, can talk about it with complete confidence and are (usually) very enthusiastic. The fact that they may be poor salespeople makes no difference as we are not talking about selling what the business offers but about telling people that the business now exists and what it offers. Any time that the principals can spend actively talking to people is almost certain to be time well spent.

Using Representatives or Agents

The use of representatives or agents will depend on a number of factors. Where few sales are required and selling is complex, there may be an absolute need to discuss all aspects of the product with the potential buyer and that may well mean employing suitable staff. Where the product is simple and can be described in an advertisement or leaflet, it is unlikely to be cost effective to call personally on every possible buyer unless the customers are wholesalers or large end-users where the volume of sales becomes important.

Having decided that representation is needed, there are two main divides: the representative or the agent.

The representative is a paid member of the staff who may or may not receive a bonus (or commission) based on results. All his running costs will be borne by the business. An agent is a freelance who meets his own costs and is paid only on results.

The advantages of using the representative are that he is devoting his entire time to selling your business and is under your total control. He is, however, expensive to run and that can become critical if he does not achieve the right results.

The agent, on the other hand, costs little to run. However, he is not dedicated to your business and may well find that other products he carries are easier to sell and ignore yours altogether.

It is never easy to decide which route to follow but, regardless of that, it is essential that all who represent the business are properly trained and able to enthuse about it, otherwise the results will be very disappointing.

The Best Salespeople

A satisfied customer is not only your best prospect but also your best representative.

It follows that time spent on ensuring that your customers are satisfied is very well worthwhile.

However, customers will only talk about you if either they are asked whether they know someone in your line of business or you do something to make yourself the subject of a conversation. You have no control over the first but you can do something about the second.

In some cases this brings us back to direct mail shots to customers. In others it requires a bit more imagination. One grocer I knew stood an enormous teddy bear at the back of his shop which was put there to help his brother-in-law who was opening a toy shop at the other end of the town. To his surprise, people talked and his own business improved. As a result he decided to make it a regular event and every week another large or eye-catching toy appeared. He calculated that this added nearly 15 per cent to his takings and, obviously, it cost him nothing. How many people would consider that putting toys in a grocer's shop would help sales? The reason was simple: it gave his customers something to talk about.

The Right Place at the Right Time
We have already seen that the person in the right place at the right time is the one who gets the business.

The only way consistently to achieve that situation is to be everywhere all the time. Clearly that is an impossible target, but the more time spent actively selling, the greater the chance of being the right person in the right place at the right time. Indeed, activity is the only way to achieve consistent results.

To that end, it should be remembered that the publican who finds the time to stop and talk to his customers is selling. He is working to ensure that the customers return again and again to his establishment rather than drifting off to a competitor down the road who is friendlier. Furthermore, he has realised that he does not just sell beer – he sells everything that makes up his business: atmosphere, comfort, companionship, relaxation, etc.

Likewise, all staff at all times when they are in contact with customers are acting as part of the sales team. They should be made aware of this fact and trained to take full advantage of those moments when they are in a prime selling position: face to face with the customer.

Many customers expect to meet the head of the business if the orders they are placing are large. There is no real reason for a meeting except to improve the rapport between that customer and the business. However, that meeting can be very important – the closer the customer feels to the business, the higher the probability that he will act as an unpaid representative who can sell the business with great authority.

9

FINANCIAL RECORDS

Introduction

The chances are that you hate the thought of administration. Most people with an entrepreneurial bent tend to be the worst administrators in the world. If this applies to you, you are going to have to come to terms with the fact that all businesses, no matter how small, must keep proper records or get into trouble.

That trouble may come from a variety of directions – the taxman if the accounting records are not kept, your customers if you do not have a system of ensuring that they get what they want when they want it, your suppliers if you fail to pay your bills, and you yourself if you suddenly find the business in deep trouble without warning.

Keeping the Inland Revenue Happy

This is a requirement for every business although how complex it will be will vary.

The record of sales will depend on whether all sales are made for cash, all by way of invoices or a combination of the two. Where all are cash sales, the basic requirement is to keep a record of all cash taken on a daily basis. Where all sales are by invoice, a list of invoices is sufficient. Both are required if both apply. Remember that the Inspector of Taxes is not concerned with whether or not your invoices have been paid – he wants to know the value of your sales. Having said that, if you end up with any 'bad debts' – invoices that are never going to be paid – the value of those invoices can be offset against your profit at the end of the year as 'bad debt provision'.

Exactly the same thing applies when considering expenditure. In theory, there is no need to analyse your expenditure in order to calculate your taxable profit. However, that is likely to lead to queries. The conventional way to separate out costs is as indicated in Chapter 4 although the details will vary.

Most small businesses start using a cash book which has one or two columns for sales at the left of the left-hand page and up to fifteen columns for expenditure spreading across the rest of the left-hand page and the right-hand page. One of these will be used to total expenditure, the rest will be headed with items of expenditure and used to analyse that expenditure.

It would be simple if we could say that the taxable profit would be the sales less the costs but that is only true if all the costs are 'tax deductible' (which means that the Inland Revenue accepts that they are genuine business costs). The areas which cause most problems with small businesses, many of which are run in whole or in part from the home, are the telephone and travelling costs.

If you had a telephone at home before you started the business, and that applies to most businesses, you cannot expect to be allowed to consider the whole telephone bill as a business expense. The amount you will be allowed to deduct will be subject to agreement with the Inspector but there are ways in which you can make sure that you end up with as fair a split as possible. It helps if you have kept previous telephone bills. If, for example, the bills in your first year of trading have totalled £1,000 and you can show that the bills for the previous year were only £100, the Inspector may agree to you allocating £900 of that account and 9/10ths of future accounts to the business. If you do not have that sort of evidence, it is probable that the most you would be able to allocate would be 4/5ths (a fairly common division). This is 1/10th less or, in this case, £100 less. That would mean you would pay about £25 more in tax.

There are two further complications to bear in mind. It may well be that the quarter prior to starting the business involved a lot of calls which were related to the business (and that can apply to other expenditure as well). Obviously these costs should be taken into consideration as well as those that apply after you have commenced trading. The safest (and most sensible) way of dealing with this is to 'start' the business when you start spending money on the business (even if, at the beginning, that money is spent on deciding whether or not to start the business) rather than when you actually open the doors for trading. An example of this was the café that Jane opened. She moved in a month before she could trade. In that month she had heavy expenditure and most of it was tax deductible. This was so obvious that it is almost certain that she would have started her accounts when she moved into the premises even though she would not be trading for the first four weeks. Was this the right time? Probably not – the right time was when she started to spend money on market research, investigating properties, etc.

The second complication arises if the telephone account in year two is substantially higher than in year one. This could be the result of the business proving successful and expanding. Let us assume it doubles to £2,000. Having agreed the 9/10ths division, there would be no difficulty in posting that proportion of the account to the business, i.e. £1,800. However, we have already seen that the average account before the business started was £100 which would indicate that the amount used for business was £1,900. The only answer is to go for the £1,900 and be prepared to argue the matter with the Inspector if it is queried. After all, just because a division has been agreed does not mean that you are bound by it. If it ceases to be right, try to get a more favourable division accepted.

Travelling creates similar problems. If you use a car to do no more than travel from home to your place of business and back again, you are not really entitled to tax relief on any of your travelling costs – after all, you are in the same position as any employee who has to drive to work and such employees are unable to claim so why should you? However, certain other uses are obviously deductible. Jane will use hers to collect goods from the cash and carry. Tradesmen will often use theirs to visit customers' homes both to look at a job and price it and to carry out the work. If selling is involved, the car will be used to visit potential customers.

Some business people work on a mileage basis, keeping a logbook showing each journey and indicating whether it was for business or pleasure. They then book all costs to the business and correct the figures at the end of the year by dividing the costs by the total mileage and multiplying them by the miles used for business. If you are prepared to be that thorough, the Inspector should accept your calculations without question. Unfortunately few of us are and my guess is that even the few that decide to use that system fail to keep it going for long. This brings us back to negotiation with the Inspector and agreeing a division. There is, however, no doubt that the better the records you keep, the more likely you are to come to a favourable agreement. The important thing is to be fair to the Inspector. You are not allowed to deduct the cost of going to your place of business or for any private motoring and if you try it on you deserve to come out with a less favourable division.

However, there are ways and means of reducing non-deductible miles. For example, if you leave home to visit a customer or potential customer or cash and carry on your way to your business premises, the whole journey is for business purposes. The same thing applies when coming home. If you are going to visit a favourite aunt, see if there is some good business reason for going in that direction.

One other matter should not be overlooked. If you use a room at home as an office, you, as occupier, are entitled to 'charge' your business for 'Use of office'. This is intended to cover a proportion of the rates and a contribution towards heating and lighting costs. A reasonable figure such as £500 per annum is unlikely to be queried and would reduce your final tax bill by just over £100 at present rates. However, if you own your home, claiming office expenses can result in Capital Gains Tax becoming payable when you sell the house – it is worth discussing this with your Inland Revenue Inspector to clarify the position.

To sum up. Record everything that you need to record and claim items about which you are in doubt but make your doubts known to the Inspector. He will take the decision in any event and will be more inclined to be on your side if you have been honest with him.

If you feel unable to handle the Inland Revenue yourself you will need to employ a book-keeper or an accountant. However, the Inspectors are very helpful and the procedures are not at all complicated. Many small business people handle their own tax affairs and save themselves the cost of using someone else. If you decide to do it all yourself, visit your local tax office and discuss your business with one of the Inspectors before you start.

Larger limited companies must have their accounts audited by a Chartered Accountant to comply with the law.

Keeping the VATman Happy
First of all, you have to decide whether or not you should be registered for VAT. Incidentally, VAT is administered and collected by HM Customs and not HM Inland Revenue.

Once your business reaches a certain turnover, registration is mandatory. The threshold is changed from time to time and you should check to find out what it is from your local HM Customs VAT office.

Below that figure it is up to you and whether or not you register will depend on a number of factors.

The concept is that businesses which are registered add VAT to their prices and owe that VAT to HM Customs. However, they are allowed to claim back from HM Customs the VAT that was charged to them on their supplies.

If you are a retailer handling goods which attract VAT and you calculate your sales prices by doubling your NET purchase prices, the calculation is as follows:

If you are registered:

	Gross	Net	VAT
To purchases	117.50	100.00	17.50
Sales price	235.00	200.00	35.00

If you are not registered:

To purchases	117.50
Sales price	217.50

In both cases you make the same profit – £100. In the first you are charging your customers £17.50 more, so there is a commercial advantage in remaining unregistered (if you are selling to the general public) as you can compete more effectively against those who are registered.

The position is even more dramatic if you are providing a service where most of your price is made up of charges for your time.

If you are registered:

	Gross	Net	VAT
To time	211.50	180.00	31.50
To supplies	23.50	20.00	3.50
	235.00	200.00	35.00

If you are not registered:

To time	180.00
To supplies	23.50
	203.50

So, when does it pay to register?

The answer is simple: when most of your customers are registered businesses who can claim back the VAT that you are charging them. In the example above, they can claim back the £35 if you are registered but not the £17.50 if you are not. This means that the competitive edge is the other way around and that you are at the disadvantage.

Whether you register on a voluntary basis or because you have to, there are certain basic records you will have to keep in order to fill in your VAT returns. The actual records needed depend on the scheme that applies to your business – details from HM Customs VAT offices.

Obviously, if you are registered it helps if you can evolve a system that covers both the usual accounts and the VAT to avoid duplicating the work involved.

Controlling the Business

This may be divided into two categories, keeping track of who owes what and ensuring that the business is progressing satisfactorily.

The Ledgers

In order to keep track of what you owe and of sums owing to you from customers you may need to create two ledgers, one for purchases and the other for sales. Whether you will need both, one or neither will depend on your particular business.

The Purchase Ledger is basically a book in which each supplier who supplies on credit terms has a page. You enter invoices on the page when they are received and payments when they are made. As a result you always know what you owe to each supplier and, by adding these figures together, the total amount that you owe.

The Sales Ledger is exactly the same but the other way round.

Incidentally, two terms you will meet that may cause some confusion are Creditors and Debtors. A Creditor is someone to whom you owe money and a Debtor is someone who owes you money.

Management Accounts

The records that you keep to ensure that the business is progressing as planned are usually called Management Accounts – because they are created for management purposes.

When we prepared Jane's Business Plan we indicated on a month by month basis what sales she predicted and all her costs – direct, fixed and overhead.

One way of dealing with the situation is to prepare a similar sheet and to post to it actual figures as soon after the end of the month as possible. These figures should not only show what has been paid but also what is being held on the purchase and sales ledgers. In other words, sales will be the actual sales for the month not the cash received (which could apply to sales in previous months) and costs will be the costs incurred not those settled.

Obviously, we hope that the actual figures will be close to

our predictions and, if they are, we know that we have little to worry about. Sales which are below prediction and costs which are higher than predicted are both danger signals telling us that something needs to be done.

Another method is to use percentages. We touched on this when we looked at the market stall. A simple way to keep track of the business is to check the actual sales figures against budget and then to compare the various actual percentages. Since most variation will be with direct costs, this is the most important. Indeed, if you are sure that the actual fixed costs are as budgeted (and they should be) and that the overheads are also more or less in line with expectations, only two figures really matter: sales and direct costs as a percentage of sales. If the sales are well above budget but the percentage spent on direct costs is too high, you may have as many problems as the person who is having difficulty in meeting his sales targets.

Whether or not your business needs to maintain management accounts must be your decision. The smaller business which is bubbling along perfectly satisfactorily can be run without keeping management accounts; always remember that there is no point in keeping these records unless you are going to use them. Believe it or not, some people keep wonderful records but never bother to check to see what the figures mean. That is a pure waste of time.

These figures will tell you whether or not you are on target to make the profits that you predict; they will not help you to check that your cashflow is in order. In Jane's case she need go little further because all her sales are against cash. Unfortunately, that does not always apply.

We have seen that a business can survive periods of small profits and even losses so long as there is sufficient cash flowing through the system to meet all the bills that have to be paid. The converse is just as true. A business can be very profitable and yet be forced to close down because the cashflow has dried up.

Your cashflow is improved when you buy goods and services on credit. It is made worse when you sell goods on credit. In practice, what happens is that the small businessman finds he has to give people credit and then, because he can no longer pay cash for goods and services, is forced to get those on credit. So far, so good. However, the day may come when you are no longer allowed as much credit as you need and so you can no longer get the goods and services you need in order to satisfy your next customer.

Most business people turn to their bank at this point and try to arrange an overdraft facility. Generally speaking, this is exactly the wrong thing to do (and banks often refuse the request for that reason). It is the wrong thing to do because it is costly. The extra costs involved in operating with an overdraft can easily absorb a high percentage of profit. The end result is that you not only have a cashflow problem but have added to it a profitability problem.

The answer is fairly simple although a lot of people find this one of the hardest parts of running a business.

Go back to your ledgers. In theory, if the total owed to your creditors is no more than the total owed to you by your debtors, you have few problems. In practice, this is a dangerous simplification. For a start you should not just compare the totals. If purchases represent 60 per cent of your sales, the purchase ledger should never carry more than 60 per cent of the total carried on the sales ledger. In other words, you should never owe more than 60 per cent of the sum you are owed. If this ceases to be true, you are living off your creditors – a situation that cannot go on for long.

Even keeping that balance right is not enough. Consider what is called 'ageing'. An account may be current (that is created in this month and not yet due for payment), due (that is created last month and due for payment this month) or overdue by so many months. Danger signals should start being lit as soon as any of your customers move into the overdue zone.

If you allow your sales ledger to get out of hand in this way, you may have to close the business even if you are theoretically doing very well. The answer is to avoid getting into that situation in the first place. In some businesses, you just have to give credit and cannot trade unless you do. That is fair enough but it needs to be controlled.

This is something that few business people are prepared to face up to but it really is not that difficult.

Start off by deciding how much you can afford to lose without it really hurting. I know that all losses hurt but every business can afford a certain amount of bad debt. Let us say we decide on £250 per customer.

That should be the absolute limit of credit that you give to an unknown new customer.

If you are asked to give more credit than that, take out references before you confirm that you have accepted the order. Some people will resent this and many starting up a business are so excited that they have captured an order that they are terrified of losing it by insisting on references. It is an almost universal truth that any customer who objects to a supplier taking up a reference will prove to be a bad payer.

Take at least two references from other suppliers. In the old days we used to take a bank reference as well but bankers are so afraid of litigation that the references they give these days aren't really worth taking. Some people ask for references and fail to take them up. Their argument is that the fact that referees have been given is enough. It isn't. Your potential customer may be relying on you taking that view. Take up the references and take note of what they say. If you have to reduce the level of credit requested, go and see the customer and explain the position. Offer to supply against cash or to supply part orders (if this is possible) which will keep the account within the level you have chosen.

Even though you have taken references, a customer may find himself in financial difficulties and fail to pay your account within the specified period. Stop supplies at once. Even if you have made something special, do not deliver it until the account is in order. If you are in the middle of making something – stop work. True, you may lose this customer but, at the end of the day, the sooner you do, the better.

The day may come when you stand the chance of an order from a local authority or a large, well-established company. In both cases there will be no doubt as to their ability to pay. In both cases it is highly likely that they have a fairly automatic payment procedure and there is nothing you can do to change it. Find out when you can expect payment – it may be as long as 120 days after date of invoice in extreme cases. Can your business afford to offer that period of credit? If not, this may well be a case for asking the bank for a short-term overdraft facility – to be used only if the contract comes your way. However, the bank will make charges for that overdraft and will also want interest on the money borrowed. Check with the bank the TOTAL cost of borrowing and build that into the cost of meeting the contract. If you come up with a price which is too high to be competitive you will have to decide whether you can afford to take a lower profit or not. If you can, well and good. If you can't, you will have to decline to quote (or tender). The important thing is that you go into the situation with your eyes open and that you have the courage to decline even the most prestigious of orders if need be.

Using a Book-Keeping Service

Many small businesses employ a book-keeping service to keep their books. This has a number of advantages.

If you are able to use the time you save, on making more profit, the service costs you nothing.

You know that your records are being kept properly.

You can choose between someone who is no more than a book-keeper or someone who has a wider range of experience. In these cases you may find that you have someone else who knows the financial side of the business as well (if not better) than you do, which means there is someone with whom you can share your ideas; someone who, while on your side, can take a critical look at your thoughts.

Some book-keepers are more than capable of dealing with both the Inland Revenue and the VAT office. However, you may decide to employ an accountant and some offer a book-keeping service within their practice.

10

ADMINISTRATION

Basic Job Administration

The main purpose of job administration is to ensure that your business operates profitably. There are two basic requirements to achieve that end.

1. To ensure that all your customers' orders are properly executed on time. If you fail in this, you will gradually find you have no customers.

2. To ensure that all work carried out is properly and promptly invoiced. Remember, when you have just satisfied a customer's needs, he is feeling grateful to you – but the 'gratitude curve' drops fairly quickly. It is far easier to get paid for work when the gratitude reading is high. An incorrect or late invoice can greatly reduce your chances of rapid settlement and we saw in the last chapter the problems that can be caused by late payment.

The first requirement varies a good deal from business to business but in all cases there must be a formal system for logging in orders received. The system should ensure that all who have to do something know what has to be done and when – and that includes the invoicing department. That describes almost exactly the system that Jane uses in her café.

When a customer gives an order, the waiter or waitress writes it down on a pad with a carbon copy. The top sheet goes to the kitchen so they know what to prepare; the bottom one goes on a clip by the till and is used to work out the bill when the customer leaves. Both carry the table number for easy identification.

When the order is for a full meal, the kitchen copy carries out a number of functions. Most kitchen 'systems' rely on the physical position of the order sheets to mark progress and indicate the next job to be done. This is usually achieved using a board with a number of bulldog clips fitted to it. Each clip carries a heading: 'Awaiting Starter', 'Awaiting Main Course', 'Eating Main Course', etc. Remember, a system does not have to be complicated to achieve what it sets out to do and the best system is the simplest system that can meet all the requirements.

It may be a good deal more complex involving many more than two people and can include worksheets for keeping track of time spent and materials and parts used, purchase requisitions if materials or parts have to be ordered, etc.

Many trades, and the motor trade is a good example, tend to standardise on systems as they all have the same requirements. In these cases you can buy a system that you know has the capability of working (whether it works or not is then up to you). In other cases, you will have to design the system yourself.

A manufacturing situation highlights most of the problems.

When an order is received a number of people need to be informed as follows:

Sales – so that they can enter details into the customer records.

Production Control – for a variety of reasons which we will come back to.

Accounts – so that they are alerted to the need to raise an invoice when the time comes.

The easiest way to ensure that all are informed is to make out a triplicate 'Job Card' where the bottom section is actually on card.

Accounts receives the top copy which indicates the price to be charged to the customer or states that this job is on a 'time and materials' basis. Sales receives the second copy. The interesting copy is the one that goes to Production Control and so we will follow that one rather more carefully.

Since we are talking about a manufacturing firm, the job will require some materials and/or parts from which it will be made.

Job 1. Find out and fill in the material requirements on the card. Pass the card to the storekeeper.

Job 2. The storekeeper checks on stocks, marks off what is available in stock (and allocates it so that it cannot be used for another job) and passes the card back to Production Control.

Job 3. Order all other requirements and indicate on the card when all materials and parts are expected to be available.

Job 4. Check how long the job will take and book it into the 'Work Diary' to start when everything is to hand. Store the card in an appropriate place.

Clearly nothing will happen until the start date arrives by which time, at least in theory, all materials, etc., are available.

Job 5. When the time comes, Production Control issues the card to the first operator who uses it to collect what he needs from the stores and to keep note of the time he spends on the job.

The card then moves with the work to Despatch who use it to make out the Despatch Note and to indicate what charges should be made for packing and delivery. The card then speeds its way back to the Accounts department.

Once the job is complete, the Accounts department 'costs' all materials, parts and labour. If the work is being carried out on a time and materials basis, that is the figure that goes on the invoice. If not, the figure is compared with the price at which the order was accepted to ensure that the costs were in line with expectations. To ensure that this information is not 'lost in the system' the Accounts copy is endorsed with the costs and passed to the Estimator for future reference. Last of all, Accounts file the Production copy away where it can be found if required.

Yes, I hear you say, that is all very well but we are a small firm with three partners and no employees. It makes no difference at all.

If you are running a one-man business you will be spending a part of each day on each function – salesman, storekeeper, production operator, invoice clerk, etc. – and you will find that it pays to use a job card set as described. Put the sales copy in a tray by the sales records until you have time to deal with it – otherwise you will forget and with the telephone ringing you really don't have time now, do you?

Rig yourself up with a row of clips on the wall. Mark them 'Awaiting Material Ordering', 'Awaiting Materials', 'Awaiting Production' and 'Awaiting Invoice', etc. You may need a number of 'Awaiting Production' clips marked 'Today', 'This Week', 'Next Week' and 'Later'.

If you make something, repair something or service something, and it doesn't matter what that 'something' is (which means it includes building works of all kinds), you will never regret inventing and using some such system.

Stock Records
If you are thinking of running any business which carries stock, you need to know how much you have at any time.

The simplest and most foolproof system is to arrange your stock so that you can see it. In my business the stock is basic stationery, letterheads, printer ink cartridges, etc. These are all kept on shelves in a cupboard so that when you open the door you can see what is running low. That is fine – especially if you can give it an 'auto-flag' system. Take photocopying paper. This is stacked on a shelf with a card giving the supplier's name, order reference and amount to order fixed on the shelf edge with a couple of drawing pins. The back of the cupboard behind the label has a 3 inch wide strip of red paint from the shelf up to the height of four reams of paper. As soon as there are only three reams left, the red stripe shows. The same thing applies to other items. It takes seconds to open the door, check the red stripes and jot down what has to be ordered.

If you can't create a visible system like this, you will have to use a record card for each item. Remember, the whole point is to ensure that (a) you never run out of a stock item and (b) you never have more on the shelf than you need as that means money unnecessarily tied up in bits and pieces. Our paper arrives the day after it is ordered. The maximum amount of paper we use in any one day is three reams. Therefore, the minimum stock is fixed at three reams. We have to order ten reams in order to receive a discount and get free delivery. That would suggest that the order quantity should be ten reams. However, every time you place an order you are incurring administration costs and this would mean buying every week. Given you have the storage space, a monthly order of about forty reams would make more sense.

If we needed to stock widgets and widget delivery was four months, our minimum stock would be the maximum number of widgets we would use in four months. The order quantity would depend on the pricing structure of widgets.

Again, the best system is the simplest that you can devise which works well and takes least time to operate.

Remembering Lessons
Most jobs teach us something – which may be something general or specific to that job.

Two examples will illustrate the point. You are a plumber and you visit a customer to deal with a WC which doesn't flush properly. Whilst you are there you need to turn off the water at the mains. The owner doesn't know where it is and you have to track it down. Eventually you find it behind a large fridge/freezer in a small larder off the kitchen. It takes you nearly half an hour to clear the way to turn off the water – and the same time to put everything back in place. All this means that the job has taken nearly an hour and a half more than you expected. This sort of information should be logged onto the customer's work record in such a way as to ensure that when you (or one of your men) return to the house a few years later, this information is available before you go. This sort of thing is especially important if you are likely to have to quote a guide price before the visit.

The second example covers a repair situation. The first time an individual repairs any given item, the chances are that the job will take far too long as the repairer finds out how best to tackle the job. Again, it pays to make notes – but this time not on the customer cards but against the item repaired. At the time this will not seem to be necessary – after all, who could forget what they have just learned? Firstly, it may be some time before the repairer is faced with the same item and secondly it may be that the work will have to be carried out by someone else for whom it is another 'first'.

This sort of record keeping is frequently ignored on the basis that it is not likely to be required. After all, who knows when the plumber may get another call out to that house? Clearly, if you *know* that you will never need the information, it is a waste of time keeping it, whilst if you *know* that you will need it, there is no argument. Unfortunately, it is yet another area where the businessperson has to take a judgment but it is worth adding that very few people regret keeping notes and records whilst many regret that they have not. When considering most aspects of administration, it is always better to create an 'overkill' situation in the early days of a business, discarding what proves pointless as time goes on.

Basic Sales Administration
Before we start selling the business, we need to put in place some form of record keeping so that we know whom we have contacted (and when), what literature they have been given or sent, what interest (if any) they showed and what follow-up action (if any) is needed.

We will look at using computers in another chapter but the manual system that follows should be perfectly adequate – if slower and more cumbersome than a computer based system.

Contact Record Cards

Every contact (or 'potential customer' if you prefer) should be given a record card and, if your contacts run businesses, one for each contact within the business, plus one for the business itself.

The card should carry as a minimum the contact's surname, forenames or initials and title (remember: some women prefer Ms to Mrs or Miss and, since you are trying to sell to them, it is not only polite but also sensible to title them as they prefer); the full address including post code (you want them to get their post the next day, don't you?); telephone number, facsimile number (if they have one and you have access to a fax) and email address (if they have one and you have access to the Internet).

Every time that person is contacted by you or contacts you – by telephone, by visit or by letter – a note is made on the record card. The note should cover everything of importance, especially if follow-up action is required. Gradually these cards build up a picture of the contact which you will find of the greatest possible assistance in your selling campaign.

These cards should be filed in alphabetical order of the surnames and should be kept near the telephone on which sales calls are taken so that you can be looking up the card as you speak. Contacts expect you to know all about them and, if you do, you are well on the way to making sales.

Incidentally, those cards in the name of a firm should be filed under the firm's name and need carry no more than a cross reference to the contact cards.

Customer Records

As soon as a 'contact' becomes a 'customer', you will need to record details of every order received. The ideal system is one which provides you with all the available information very quickly indeed. If that can be achieved, when a customer telephones you, you can make them feel that you have actually remembered everything about them – even if the last contact was a couple of years ago. Not only does this demonstrate your professionalism, it also vastly increases your chance of further work from that customer.

Many people just use the reverse side of the Contact Card for order details, etc. There is absolutely nothing wrong with that unless you need something more complicated.

Customer records are the key to direct mail shots. They are particularly valuable in the hotel trade. Your records reveal that, over the last five years, you have been host to 146 couples who have been on holiday with you outside the main season, all of whom have been interested in, let us say, visiting historic houses and gardens. You decide to run a special four day spring break, including coach visits on the two central days to two houses whose gardens are famous for their spring bulb displays. Thanks to the way in which you keep notes about customers you have easily identified those who might be interested and, since you can only accommodate 18 couples, calculate that you need 12.3 per cent of the couples in your records. You price the weekend so that it would be profitable if only 12 couples arrived, send off a 'personal' invitation to all those on your list and await results. The chances are that you will have a full hotel when all the others around you are empty – all because you keep good customer records.

We have already seen that using direct mail to customers is a cost effective way of promoting new products or services. It can work only if suitable records are kept and ceases to be cost effective if those records do not enable you to 'target' your direct mail as indicated above. Sending the letter to all the hotel customers would have cost so much that the whole exercise would have been unprofitable.

Sales Action System
One way of ensuring that you actually do what you have promised to do is to keep the contact's record card out of the system and put it somewhere which means 'Action'. I know a number of business people who do that and I think it is a very bad system indeed.

For a start, the card is no longer where it belongs so cannot be found quickly if needed. Secondly, it is liable to get lost.

A much better system is to use a simple duplicate book – probably the A5 size. When action is required, note it in the book. Then note the page number on the contact record card. Lastly, tear out the top copy and put that in your action clip or on your desk or whatever it is you do with bits of paper that need to be dealt with. When the job, whatever it may be, has been done, make a note on the duplicate sheet in the action book. If things go wrong (and they will), you then have a permanent record to which you can refer. Incidentally, it pays to fold that duplicate sheet back onto itself when the action is completed. That way you know that the sheets that are still unfolded are saying 'don't forget'.

The action system should also cater for the possibility of creating further sales – if you can remember to contact the customer at the right time or following a given event.

The first is fairly obvious. You run a business servicing oil-fired boilers. These need to be attended to once every twelve months. A simple diary system is all you require. The same system works when the customer buys 'consumables'. You need to know the average rate at which the items you supply are used so as to be able to contact the customer when he is due to re-order.

The second point probably requires a bit more explanation and only applies to a small minority of businesses. It falls into two categories: specific and general.

The specific is demonstrated by a wine merchant supplying to local hotels, clubs, etc. The main competition is the 'Cash and Carry' who can usually undercut his prices but, unlike him, does not offer a free delivery service or, and this can be important, free glassware for functions. If he can get prior warning whenever one of his customers is about to hold a function, he can approach them to discuss their requirements at the right moment.

An example of the more general is the plumber who knows which of his customers are likely to have problems following a period of intense cold.

Advertising Records
All advertising and media publicity should be recorded with the costs incurred and details of the results achieved. This is because we want to make sure that our advertising budget is

being spent sensibly and that means we need to know how cost effective every advertisement was.

The cost effectiveness of any form of sales is calculated by dividing the sales achieved by the costs incurred.

Whilst it is easy to keep a record of advertisements placed (more record cards), it is far harder to keep track of responses to those advertisements. A degree of accuracy can be achieved by spacing out advertisements both on a time basis and on an area basis, although some responses will occur long after the advertisement appeared and some people see regional press in other areas. Even so, it will give a fair indication of the position.

Another way is to ask people making enquiries how they heard about the business. This works well – provided people remember to ask, note down the answer and pass it on to whoever is keeping the records.

As enquiries come in, note how many have been received on the advertisement record card (the easiest way is to keep the figure in pencil so that it can be altered easily). By dividing the cost by the number of enquiries we know the cost per enquiry. Although enquiries are not orders, it is helpful to be able to compare these figures – especially in the early days when orders are thin on the ground.

As orders come in, the same applies, except that you note not only the number of orders but also the value. Then you can calculate both the cost per order and the 'cost effectiveness' of the advertisement.

The results may surprise you. One of my clients ran two advertising campaigns but kept no records. One was in 'the local rag' and cost him £12 an issue (being on a contract rate) for 52 issues. Total cost £624 (plus VAT but you can ignore that as he was VAT registered). The other went out four times a year to a specific glossy magazine although he admitted he would have liked to have been in it every month. Each advertisement cost him £120 – cost per annum being £480. Thus his total advertising cost for the year was £1,104.

We started to keep records. In the next six months, the local rag generated 262 orders with a total gross profit of £3,668 whilst the glossy produced 196 orders with a total gross profit of £3,828 (£7,496 for the half year). The corresponding cost effectiveness figures (based in this case on gross profit rather than turnover) were 11.76 and 15.95 (gross profit divided by half the annual cost as the period was for six months). Remember, the higher the figure, the better the advertising is doing.

Result – he stopped advertising locally, spent £1,440 less a 15 per cent contract discount (net £1,224) with the glossy which added £120 to his advertising budget. Based on the cost effectiveness figure, this should have resulted in orders producing a gross profit of 720 × 15.95 = £11,484 being received in the next six months. (Note that the 15.95 was calculated on the gross cost and so the 15 per cent discount must be ignored.) In fact, the final figure was £14,386 because he benefited from the 'repetition factor'. New cost effectiveness factor, 23.5 (this time using half the discounted cost) which is virtually double the CE factor for the local rag. More importantly, his gross profit was nearly doubled for an increased outlay of only £120.

Filing
Filing cabinets are expensive but you must have some sort of order or you will never find what you want. As far as letters (sent and received) are concerned, I still use a very simple system that I started well over twenty years ago. All letters are given a number and put on top of a pile in a drawer in my desk. To find the next number, simply open the drawer and see what the last one was. These numbers were then noted on the record cards (contact, customer, supplier, etc.). I say 'were' because I now use a computer and the records are held on a database. However, the principle is exactly the same.

Obviously, sooner or later the desk drawer becomes full up. I then take the bottom half out and store them away in simple box files. By keeping the drawer half full I very rarely have to refer back to these box files which, including the ones now up in the loft, hold a complete record of letters from day one.

Eventually, the record card (or database entry) is full. When I kept record cards, the important details were transferred to a new card and the old card filed, taking the next file number, with that file number noted on the new card. Now I print out the information from the database, file the printout and erase the details from the database.

Although crude, the three big advantages are that you can find a letter (from the record card entry) while on the telephone, you do not end up with heaps of papers waiting to be filed (which is when you need them most and have least chance of finding them) and there is no need to buy expensive filing equipment. If there are any disadvantages I have yet to find them, although I will admit that the system breaks down completely if you forget to put the letter number on the record.

11

RAISING FINANCE

Introduction

It is probable that at some time you will need to borrow some money. Most people approach a lender looking at their loan requirement from their own point of view. Whilst this is natural, it is obviously sensible to look at the same application from the potential lender's side of the fence to ensure that it stands a reasonable chance of being acceptable. So how do lenders look at loan applications? They look at three basic considerations when they receive an application for a commercial loan – the project, the people behind the project (and their resources) and the lending market of the day.

Lenders are always seeking what they perceive to be sensible projects – we shall look at the definition of a sensible project later – and this never varies.

Lenders want to be sure that the people behind the project have what it takes to make a success of the project – another matter that never varies and to which we shall return.

The lending market of the day is the main variable. At any given time, lenders will be willing to fund certain 'market sectors' and not others. This reflects their general view as to the strength of those market sectors at the time of the application. It has been said that lenders will lend when a market sector is flourishing – and so about to go into decline – but not when it is stagnating – and so about to thrive. Sadly, there is an element of truth behind this somewhat cynical view but all business people can do is to hope that the lending market is favourable to them and their project when they need finance.

A Sensible Proposal

A Sensible Proposal has Adequate Cashflow leading to ulti-mate profitability
One of the first things to consider about any project is cashflow. This must be capable of supporting all requirements until – and after – the profitability is reached.

A business can survive for quite long periods even though it is not making a profit, so long as there is sufficient cash flowing through the system to pay all the bills. Even so, profitability must be the ultimate aim.

As we have seen, unless you are familiar with a given market sector it can be quite difficult to estimate probable cashflow profiles and profit expectations and you cannot hope to do that without carrying out a good deal of homework. Apart from the fact that you ought to do this for your own peace of mind, it is extremely unreasonable to ask for a loan unless you have carried out adequate research. Otherwise the applicant deserves rejection – which is what usually happens.

As we have seen, we do not really know the answer until we have carried out a full financial analysis on the project to establish (as accurately as possible) cashflow forecasts and estimated profit and loss accounts and this really is an essential exercise.

A Sensible Proposal operates in a Sensible Market Place
The lender will expect you to provide adequate evidence that there is sufficient demand in the market place in which the business is to operate.

A Sensible Proposal is not Over Geared
Gearing is loosely defined as the ratio of borrowed money to the total money required for a given project.

Generally speaking, most businesses are set up using a cash input – which may be in part from the founders and in part from others (investors – people who are prepared to put up some cash but will not be active in the business) – and some debt finance (borrowed money). The investors will expect some return on their investment but there is no commitment to

provide that return. If a favourite aunt is prepared to put
£5,000 into your business as an investment, she is offering you
'risk capital' – i.e. cash which she hopes will make her a
return but which she fully understands is 'at risk' if the
business does not succeed.

Almost every project can carry a certain amount of debt
finance but, unlike the cash input, debt *has* to be serviced.
Depending on the nature of the loan, servicing will always
include paying the agreed interest charges when they fall due
and may include paying off the capital in accordance with
some agreement. To that extent, commercial loans operate in
much the same way as a domestic mortgage. The lender may
agree to accept interest only on condition that some mechanism (such as an endowment policy) is in force to repay the
capital after an agreed number of years. In other cases, the
lender expects to receive capital with each interest payment,
just like a capital repayment mortgage. The main difference is
that some lenders will offer a 'capital holiday' – a period
during which interest alone is paid – before the capital
repayments start. This is done to help a business during the
early years.

The amount of debt that any business can stand is determined by the financial analysis but, as a rule of thumb, if the
debt finance exceeds 60 per cent of the total project costs it
will be over-geared and many lenders will expect debt finance
to be no more than 50 per cent of the total project cost.

A Sensible Proposal offers Sufficient Security to Lenders
All lenders will require some sort of security, usually in the
form of property.

As far as straightforward lending is concerned, few lenders
will offer more than 70 per cent of the value that they place on
the security. Unfortunately, lenders do not all look at security
value the same way.

Some compare the loan to the 'Bricks and Mortar' value of
the property without taking into consideration any business
carried on from the property. The difficulty with this type of
approach is that highly specialised buildings (hospitals, nurs-
ing homes, theatres, petrol filling stations, etc.) have little or

no value without the business for which they were designed.

Others are more concerned with the 'Going Concern Value', which is the value of the property plus the value of the business operated from that property. Again, there are problems – especially when the business value is largely dependent on the individual or a group of individuals (as with public houses where the personalities involved really make up the business).

As a result, some lenders think in terms of 'Open Market Value' which is the purchase price that could be attained in a 'reasonable' timescale if the business were offered for sale (reasonable being usually three or six months).

Lastly, there is the 'Forced Sale Value' which is really the purchase price that would be attained if the property were auctioned following a reasonable advertising campaign.

Leasehold premises offer little security and virtually none unless the remaining term is at least fifteen years.

It is not surprising that these various approaches result in a good deal of confusion. The following can be no more than a guide but is generally as good a rule of thumb as you will get:

> The loan will never exceed 70 per cent of the Going Concern Value.
> The loan will never exceed 100 per cent of the Bricks and Mortar Value.

It is possible to raise more than the above when lenders are willing to look at additional funding in return for some form of additional security such as a charge over a domestic property, but I have dealt with the disadvantages of that one in Chapter 6.

A Sensible Project is Sensibly Planned
The lender will expect the applicants to have a planned business strategy for a period which varies but will normally cover at least three years.

This can be demonstrated only by providing the lender with a properly constructed Business Plan but, according to one lender, out of every fifty Business Plans that he sees only two are properly constructed. As you would expect, each case is judged on its merits and the strengths and weaknesses of any case may not be discernible until a thorough investigation has been carried out.

The Applicants

Skills and Experience

You would expect applicants to have the skills and experience needed to operate the proposed business but many have neither. For some reason, almost everybody thinks that they can run a business such as a public house, restaurant, guest house, small hotel or shop, even though they have had absolutely no previous experience. This is just not true.

The applicants' experience and skills need not be 'straight line' nor need they come from one person. For example, someone who has come out of the army having been running an army mess against a budget has some of the skills needed to run a restaurant. At the very least, where applicants are intending to branch out into something new to them, they should have attended all the relevant courses to provide the skills needed, although they will still lack experience. However, a combination of the successful conclusion of appropriate courses plus evidence of achievement and success in other fields of endeavour should suffice.

Character

The lender is looking for applicants who will be successful – and that means applicants who are able to cope when things are going wrong as well as when they are going right.

This is one of the main reasons why many lenders insist on meeting the applicants before coming to a decision.

Cash Availability

Many applicants have an idea and yet have absolutely no cash available to support the project. They seem to think that it is reasonable to expect other people to provide all the funds – and take all the risks – while the applicant takes all the profits (if any). Put like that – this concept is obviously not acceptable and no lender will fund 100 per cent of any project.

Applying for a Commercial Loan

Formulating the Application

The first job is to formulate an application which is likely to prove successful. That means one which meets all the above requirements and it may well not be what you want. If, for example, someone was hoping to borrow £26,000 from a bank to set up a business which, in itself, offered no security to the bank (such as a business to be run from a property on a short lease), he would have to offer the bank alternative security. Assuming that everything else is in order and he has enough equity (i.e. value of house less mortgage) in his home, he will probably get his loan. However, if the bank considers that the equity in the house is only £25,000 and they are prepared to lend up to 60 per cent of that, the most he will be offered is £15,000.

The applicant may well have to rethink his entire project under these circumstances and look for a smaller operation which is within his grasp.

Preparing the Loan Application Documentation

Having formulated a suitable application, the second job is to document it in a way that is acceptable to the bank. As has been mentioned, very few loan applications are properly documented. This does not mean to say that a badly documented application will fail – it is to say that a well-documented one is far more likely to succeed. If you wander into a bank and explain that you want a loan to start a business, they will probably give you some literature which will include some guidance as to how they want you to present your case. This guidance covers their minimum requirements and is deliberately kept as simple as possible. However, a manager will interview you and will prepare a report on your behalf. If at that interview you forget to mention something of importance, your chances of success are clearly reduced. The best way to ensure that this does not happen is to prepare your own documents or, if you are not happy to do that, get help from someone who can do the job for you.

Unfortunately, a word of warning is needed at this point. A lot of mortgage brokers, commercial consultants and accountants will agree to prepare a Business Plan (as it is usually called) on your behalf and will make a handsome charge for doing the work. Not all will know what they are doing and care needs to be exercised in choosing the right concern. As in all areas of life, a previous contented client is the best reference. Always ask if you can be given names and addresses of two clients for whom the concern has acted in preparing a Business Plan for loan application purposes and then go and talk to those two clients. There is no other way of ensuring that the costs will be well spent.

It is, of course, cheaper to do it yourself. The following is the format that I have been using for many years.

The Business Plan

Section 1. The Loan
This section introduces the project, details the loan required (amount and term) and the financial contribution from the applicants.

Section 2. The Business
This section outlines the history of the business (if applicable).

Section 3. The Project
This section provides the fullest possible details of the project.

Section 4. Security Valuations
This section provides details of the security available, estimated values and the source of such estimates.

Section 5. Project Location
This section describes the location of the project and details relevant facilities in the area, communications, etc.

Section 6. Marketing
This section covers the target markets, market research and marketing strategy.

Section 7. The Applicants
This section describes the applicants and gives background information on all key directors and managers.

Section 8. Management and Staff
This section indicates the management structure to be employed and details of the staff required.

Section 9. Contractors and Consultants
This section introduces external companies involved in any development work or employed on an ongoing basis – including bankers, accountants, solicitors, etc.

Section 10. Historic Accounting Information
Applicable only to existing businesses, this section provides details of recent trading – audited accounts being supplied as additional documentation.

Section 11. Cashflow Considerations
This section verbalises the arguments used to create the Financial Analysis. Each profit centre (actual or potential) is considered individually and the probable cash input and direct costs are explained. Staff costs, overhead costs, any development costs and the costs of servicing the loan are also covered in this section.

Section 12. Financial Analysis
This section is in the form of spreadsheets. Each profit centre is analysed and the resulting net cash surplus calculated. The cost of development works, staff costs and indirect costs are also quantified. Finally these are brought together in a 'consolidated cashflow forecast' and a 'projected profit and loss account'.

I add a few refinements to the above, such as projected balance sheets, but these are not really needed in most cases and are rather complicated.

12

JANE'S BUSINESS PLAN

You will remember that Jane needed just under £30,000 to start her business. As she had only £15,000 to put into the project this posed a problem. After discussing her plans with her husband, they agreed that they were both willing to put their house up as security for a loan to raise the difference.

There are two ways of raising funds against a domestic residence. One is to remortgage the house so as to raise the amount required. The other is to seek a loan from a bank which is secured against the house by way of a second charge. Which route is the best will depend on the lending market of the day. Generally speaking, a remortgage will be cheaper – the interest rate is likely to be lower – but there are times when building societies are not offering remortgages for business loans (because they are short of funds for their mainstream business which is lending money to enable people to buy houses). Likewise, there are times when banks are actively seeking to lend in this sort of situation and so the bank interest rate may be no more than the building society rate. To make matters worse, most building societies now have bank status. The only sound advice is to shop around when the time comes.

Whilst shopping around, don't forget to compare 'redemption penalties' or the costs involved in redeeming a loan. In Jane's case she needs the money for about six years so will set up a eight year loan to be on the safe side. If she and her husband remortgage, the 'term' will be whatever is left on her mortgage (which could be fifteen years). It could be that even with a lower interest rate offered by the building society, the cost of paying interest on the full amount for five years plus a redemption penalty make the loan more expensive than a flexible repayment arrangement with the bank where interest is paid only on the outstanding amount.

In both cases a Business Plan should be prepared and the cost of borrowing included in that plan. We will assume that Jane decided to take a 'Business Development Loan' from the bank and that the term would be five years. She had been given a table so that she could work out the repayments when she knew exactly how much she would need to borrow.

This is the Business Plan that she prepared.

THE PLAN

1.   The Loan

1.1   A loan is required in order to create a café which will appeal to local shoppers, business people and visiting tourists.

1.2   The intention is to provide beverages and snacks during the mornings; lunches; and beverages, snacks and cream teas during the afternoons.

1.3   The total cash required is £* of which £15,000 is available from savings.

1.4   The loan required is £* over a period of 8 years.

(Note: Jane is not trying to write a book but to list what matters. At this stage she does not know how much the project will cost or when the loan can be repaid (even though she is assuming, for now, that it can be done in 8 years). This is because the calculations we have already carried out ignore financial costs

(loan interest and repayments). These figures will be known when we have finished the financial calculations and can then be inserted.)

2. **The Business**

2.1   Although no business is being acquired, the property available was once used as a restaurant (which is why it has the right planning permissions and accommodation).

2.2   It was open lunchtimes and evenings but not during the morning or afternoon.

2.3   It closed over a year ago. At that time the lease expired and the owners wanted to sell the property and would not renew the lease.

2.4   From memory and from discussions with other people, the restaurant was very busy during lunchtimes and fairly busy in the evenings.

2.5   The property has been acquired by a firm of architects who wish to use the upper floors for offices and rent out the ground floor.

(Note: Some of this information may not be relevant but the more notes the better.)

3. **Property**

3.1   The property is available on a full repairing lease. The initial lease is for three years during which time the rent remains fixed.

3.2   The main shop area, approached through a central door, will accommodate eight 4-person tables and four 2-person tables.

3.3   The kitchen is adequate and complies with the required regulations.

3.4   There is ample storage in a room opening off the kitchen.

3.5   The cloakroom facilities open from the shop and include toilets for both males and females.

3.6   All main services are available and all internal services required are in place and generally very suitable.

3.7   The premises need to be redecorated and the lighting changed. This will involve some electrical work.

3.8   There are no fitting, fixtures, plant or equipment. An inventory of requirements is available if required.

3.9   It is estimated that the first month following signing the lease will be needed to carry out the refurbishment and installation of equipment, etc.

(Note: This section should be as short as possible but all the main features should be mentioned so that the reader has a fair understanding of the project and the premises from which the project will operate.)

4.   Security Valuations

4.1   It is understood that the above premises offer inadequate security.

4.2   A second charge over a domestic residence is available. The residence is presently valued at some £160,000 and carries a mortgage of £78,000.

4.3   The above valuation is based on advice taken from a local estate agent.

(Note: *If, by chance, a similar house in the locality has been sold recently, it is better to base your valuation on the sale price achieved and state that this is the way you have valued your house.)*

5.   Project Location

5.1   The premises are located at the southern end of the High Street in Lower Street.

5.2   This location is convenient for those shoppers who have parked in the car park at the end of the High Street (all of whom walk past the premises to reach their cars) and is local to a number of offices.

5.3   Many visitors congregate in this area as the coaches park almost opposite, from which point the premises are clearly visible.

6.   Marketing

6.1   Target Markets

6.1.1   Shoppers: mainly women and retired couples for morning coffees and afternoon teas.

6.1.2   Business People: mainly for lunch but some do take coffee and tea outside, especially those working in smaller shops.

6.1.3   Visitors: mainly for morning coffee and afternoon teas except at weekends when lunches become important.

6.2   Market Research

6.2.1   Having spoken to a lot of people that I know, I find that there is a general feeling that there is nowhere to have a simple lunch except in some of the pubs and one café at the other end of the town (The Red Room).

6.2.2   There are four small cafés and one bistro offering morning coffees. The bistro and one café cater for the younger, rougher element and are avoided by the women shoppers and most of the business people. The other three cafés do a good morning coffee business and it is difficult to find a seat in the middle of the morning.

6.2.3   One is vegetarian and so does not offer general lunches. One serves very expensive lunches and is used by a number of regulars who more or less freeze out anyone else. The Red Room is a direct competitor but is at the other end of the town.

6.2.4   Only the vegetarian café, The Red Room and the bistro stay open during the afternoons. The Red Room is very busy though it is off the map as far as visitors are concerned.

6.3   Marketing Strategy

6.3.1   As a good deal of money will be spent on fitting out the kitchen and the café, all those suppliers will be asked to support taking a full page spread in the local newspaper, part editorial and part advertising. The paper's advertising manager tells me that the page will cost £1,100 and has space for 12 advertisements. This means that if I can 'sell' one space to each advertiser for £110, I can have a double space for the café free of charge. (Both prices plus VAT.)

6.3.2   A leaflet drop to all the businesses in the town. The printer wants £120 plus VAT for enough A5 leaflets and the family and I can deliver them. Each leaflet can carry a voucher offering 75p off two lunches.

6.3.3   A leaflet drop to all hotels, guest houses and bed & breakfast establishments in and near the town. These would be intended for display to tell visitors about the café and would need to be in colour. The quote received for enough leaflets is £325 plus VAT and again these would be distributed by myself and by the family.

(Note: In many ways this is the most important section in the plan and it should be treated as such. Don't be tempted either to overstate the potential market or to understate the competition. Lenders are not idiots and a local bank manager who knows the locality would not be impressed.)

7.   The Applicant

7.1   Mrs Jane Maxwell (48).

7.2   Prior to having children, I worked in various restaurants as waitress, cook and manageress.

7.3   As the children grew up I worked in a local café on a part-time basis, partly as waitress and partly looking after the book-keeping side of the business.

7.4   For the last three years, until I stopped work to research this business, I have increased my hours in that café and act as manageress for the morning and lunchtime sessions and assist with buying and book-keeping two afternoons each week.

(Note: Where applicable a full CV should be included. However, in this case the above notes should be sufficient.)

8.   Management and Staff

8.1   I shall manage the business and be responsible for marketing, buying and overall control.

8.2   I intend to employ a cook/chef who would be responsible to me for all kitchen activities. He or she would have two kitchen assistants who would work shifts and be responsible for the preparation of morning snacks and afternoon teas. The shift system would ensure that both assistants are available during the lunchtime period.

8.3   I intend to employ two waiters/waitresses also working shifts so that both are available during the lunchtime period.

8.4   During the summer season, the additional staff requirements would be met in part by permanent staff working overtime and in part by casual, part-time labour.

9.   Contractors and Consultants

9.1   I intend to open a business account with my present bankers, *.

9.2   My solicitor is Mr. * of Messrs. *.

9.3   I have yet to appoint an accountant and, in view of my book-keeping experience, may well decide to deal with the Inland Revenue personally. However, I have indicated accountancy fees in my cashflow forecasts in case I find one is required.

(Note: Section 10 – mentioned in the previous chapter – is ignored since there is no existing business and subsequent section numbers have been adjusted accordingly.)

10.   Cashflow Considerations

10.1   Morning Session Sales

10.1.1   I estimate that the number of people I will serve during the weekday morning sessions will be 60 during the winter and 80 during the summer. I am assuming summer to be June, July and August. During May and September, the shoulder seasons, I have based my calculations on 70 people.

10.1.2   I estimate that each person would spend an average of 95p on beverages and 65p on sundries (biscuits, etc.).

10.1.3   On Saturday mornings I would expect the sales potential to equal this figure as, although there are fewer business people around, there are more shoppers.

10.1.4   When open on Sundays (from May to September), I would expect the sales potential to be 60 per cent of the above.

10.2   *Lunchtime Sales*

10.2.1   The number of people that could be served during the two-hour sessions is 80.

10.2.2   I estimate the average spend to be £4.30 during the week dropping to £3.50 on Saturdays and, when open, £2.50 on Sundays.

10.3   *Afternoon Sales*

10.3.1   I estimate that the maximum number of people I will serve during the afternoon sessions will be 80 in summer dropping to 70 during the shoulder season and 60 during the winter.

10.3.2   I estimate that each person would spend an average of £1.80.

10.3.3   I would expect these sales to be consistent throughout the week.

10.4   Overall Sales

10.4.1   The above equates to an annual sales potential of £161,146.

10.4.2   However, I would not expect this potential to be realised even when the business becomes established. I have based all calculations on achieving 75 per cent of the above figure providing an annual sales prediction of £120,860.

10.4.3   Obviously these figures will not be achieved in the first ycar and the estimated sales for that year are indicated in the Financial Analysis.

10.5   Direct Costs

10.5.1   The direct costs (being the cost of raw materials required) have been calculated by production of all menu items and so should prove accurate.

10.5.2   The resulting figure is 35 per cent of sales.

10.6   Staff Costs

10.6.1   Based on the staff profile above, the annual cost is £52,004 including employer's NI contributions.

10.6.2   Owing to the seasonal nature of the business, the monthly costs will be £3,909 during the low season and £4,928 from May to September.

10.7   Fixed Costs

10.7.1   These have been established as follows:

Rentals	4,850
Business Rates	1,940
General Insurance	875
Vehicle Tax and Insurance	500

10.7.2   Accordingly, the sum of £8,165 per annum or £680 per month has been allowed to meet these costs.

10.8   *Overhead Costs*

10.8.1   These have been estimated as follows:

Telephone	460
Travelling Costs	700
Stationery (including leaflets)	575
Postage	184
Repairs and Renewals	575
Advertising	600
Sundries	525
Bank Charges	575
Accountant	980

10.8.2   Accordingly, the sum of £5,174 per annum or £431 per month has been allowed to cover these costs.

10.8.3   It should be noted that travelling costs cover collection of goods from the cash and carry.

(Note: Where a specific figure looks unusually high (or low) for any reason a short explanation as in 10.8.3 is useful.)

10.9   *Ingoings*

10.9.1   A quotation has been received from the solicitor to act in checking the lease in the sum of £400.

10.9.2   The owners of the property are calling for a premium of £575.

10.9.3   Following receipt of various estimates, the sum of £2,750 has been allowed for the refurbishment programme.

10.10   *Fixtures and Fittings, Plant and Equipment*

10.10.1   It has been decided to purchase secondhand goods where possible and the overall cost reflects this decision.

10.10.2   The amount allowed is £9,500.

10.10.3   A fully costed inventory is available if required.

10.11   *Stock*

10.11.1   The use of local retailers for fresh goods and the local cash and carry for most other items reduces the cost of the initial stock.

10.11.2   The amount allowed is £1,750 – allocated in month 2.

10.11.3   A fully costed stock sheet is available if required.

10.12   *Financial Costs*

10.12.1   It is assumed that the interest rate charged will be 8 per cent although it is understood that this may not be the case.

10.12.2   It is further assumed that any loan would be repaid monthly on a capital and interest payment basis.

10.12.3   A figure of 3 per cent of the loan required has been allocated to cover any loan acquisition costs such as valuation fees and/or lender's fees.

10.13   *Personal Drawings*

10.13.1   It is my intention to take £575 per month from the business on a regular basis if this proves possible.

(Note: Although it is tedious, the above enables the lender
to understand the reasoning behind all the costings.
Some figures may be acceptable – some may not.
Where they are not, because the basis of the calcula-
tions has been explained the lender can easily adjust
the final figures to suit his assumptions.)

11.   Financial Analysis

The financial analysis comprises Spreadsheet 1 (see
page 50) plus the new spreadsheets numbered 4, 5
and 6.

(Note: It was the first year forecast (Spreadsheet 5) which
finally determined the amount of the loan Jane
needed. She found this by trial and error. To start
with she knew she needed to borrow at least £29,500
(from Spreadsheet 2) less her £15,000 which is
£14,500 but she also knew it would have to be higher
than that to cover her financial costs. She worked
out the figures based on borrowing £16,500 but
when she looked at the bottom line – the cash
surplus carried forward – she found this was nega-
tive in some months. Clearly it had to be higher.

Her second attempt was based on £18,000. This
time there were no negative figures but the lowest
surplus was quite high and she was sure she could
manage on less.

When she finished all her calculations, she went
back and completed the first section of her Business
Plan indicating that the total amount required is
£32,500 and therefore the loan required is £17,500.)

Conclusion
It is very tedious to carry out the calculations all over again.
After all, we have now been over substantially the same
ground three times – although each time for a different reason.
Nevertheless, this three-stage approach is the right way to
tackle the problems. The first was to ensure that the proposal

SPREADSHEET 4 Gross Profit (or Operating Surplus) for Year One

	Apr	May	Jun	Jul	Aug	Sep	Oct	Nov	Dec	Jan	Feb	Mar	Totals
Predicted Gross Profit	5,475.60	7,067.29	8,503.56	8,677.50	8,803.86	6,949.22	5,475.60	5,551.65	5,700.83	5,475.60	5,101.20	5,776.88	78,558.77
Adjustment for year 1 trading	0%	30%	60%	90%	90%	50%	60%	70%	80%	90%	100%	100%	
CASH INFLOW	0.00	2,120.19	5,102.14	7,809.75	7,923.47	3,474.61	3,285.36	3,886.16	4,560.66	4,928.04	5,101.20	5,776.88	53,968.44

NOTE: The business will not progress in a steady fashion because as far as the tourists are concerned this is not a new business – hence the higher figures for June, July and August.

SPREADSHEET 5 Consolidated Cashflow Forecast for Year One

	Apr	May	Jun	Jul	Aug	Sep	Oct	Nov	Dec	Jan	Feb	Mar	Totals
CASH INFLOW													
By loan	17,500.00												
By cash	15,000.00												
Operating Surplus	0.00	2,120.19	5,102.14	7,809.75	7,923.47	3,474.61	3,285.36	3,886.16	4,560.66	4,928.04	5,101.20	5,776.88	53,968.44
Total Cash Inflow	32,500.00	2,120.19	5,102.14	7,809.75	7,923.47	3,474.61	3,285.36	3,886.16	4,560.66	4,928.04	5,101.20	5,776.88	86,468.44
CASH OUTFLOW													
Ingoings	3,725.00												3,725.00
Fixtures, Fittings, etc	9,500.00												9,500.00
Initial Stock		1,750.00											1,750.00
Personal Drawings	575.00	575.00	575.00	575.00	575.00	575.00	575.00	575.00	575.00	575.00	575.00	575.00	6,900.00
Staff Costs	4,928.08	4,928.08	4,928.08	4,928.08	4,928.08	4,928.08	3,909.08	3,909.08	3,909.08	3,909.08	3,909.08	3,909.08	48,094.92
Fixed Costs	680.00	680.00	680.00	680.00	680.00	680.00	680.00	680.00	680.00	680.00	680.00	680.00	8,160.00
Overhead Costs	431.00	431.00	431.00	431.00	431.00	431.00	431.00	431.00	431.00	431.00	431.00	431.00	5,172.00
Loan Acquisition Costs	525.00												525.00
Loan Repayments	189.43	189.43	189.43	189.43	189.43	189.43	189.43	189.43	189.43	189.43	189.43	189.43	2,273.16
Total Cash Outflow	15,625.43	8,553.51	6,803.51	6,803.51	6,803.51	6,803.51	5,784.51	5,784.51	5,784.51	5,784.51	5,784.51	5,784.51	86,100.08
NET CASH INFLOW	16,874.57	(6,433.33)	(1,701.38)	1,006.24	1,119.96	(3,328.91)	(2,499.15)	(1,898.36)	(1,223.85)	(856.47)	(683.31)	(7.64)	368.37
Cash Surplus C/Fwd	16,874.57	10,441.24	8,739.87	9,746.10	10,866.06	7,537.16	5,038.00	3,139.65	1,915.79	1,059.32	376.01	368.37	

SPREADSHEET 6 Consolidated Cashflow Forecast for Year Two

	Apr	May	Jun	Jul	Aug	Sep	Oct	Nov	Dec	Jan	Feb	Mar	Totals
CASH INFLOW													
Operating Surplus	5,475.60	7,067.29	8,503.56	8,677.50	8,803.86	6,949.22	5,475.60	5,551.65	5,700.83	5,475.60	5,101.20	5,776.88	78,558.77
CASH OUTFLOW													
Personal Drawings	575.00	575.00	575.00	575.00	575.00	575.00	575.00	575.00	575.00	575.00	575.00	575.00	6,900.00
Staff Costs	3,909.08	4,928.08	4,928.08	4,928.08	4,928.08	4,928.08	3,909.08	3,909.08	3,909.08	3,909.08	3,909.08	3,909.08	52,004.00
Fixed Costs	680.00	680.00	680.00	680.00	680.00	680.00	680.00	680.00	680.00	680.00	680.00	680.00	8,160.00
Overhead Costs	431.00	431.00	431.00	431.00	431.00	431.00	431.00	431.00	431.00	431.00	431.00	431.00	5,172.00
Loan Repayments	189.43	189.43	189.43	189.43	189.43	189.43	189.43	189.43	189.43	189.43	189.43	189.43	2,273.16
Total Cash Outflow	5,784.51	6,803.51	6,803.51	6,803.51	6,803.51	6,803.51	5,784.51	5,784.51	5,784.51	5,784.51	5,784.51	5,784.51	74,509.16
NET CASH INFLOW	(308.91)	263.77	1,700.05	1,873.99	2,000.35	145.70	(308.91)	(232.86)	(83.69)	(308.91)	(683.31)	(7.64)	4,049.61
Cash Surplus C/Fwd	59.45	323.28	2,023.27	3,897.26	5,897.61	6,043.31	5,734.40	5,501.53	5,417.84	5,108.93	4,425.62	4,417.98	

would make a profit. The second was to see whether or not we could fund the start up period out of our own cash resources. The third, which uses figures already calculated (which means much of the work has been done already) is to enable us to raise a loan. As a result, it takes into consideration two matters we were able to ignore in the previous two sets of calculations – the costs of borrowing the money and of obtaining the loan. It is sometimes quite surprising how these increase the total amount needed.

In any case, you need to be able to demonstrate to a lender that as much care and trouble has been taken as is needed if you are to convince him that you are a 'sensible person' to whom a loan should be made.

13

THE OUTWARD SHOW

Image

Having decided that you wish to start the business, that it will make the profits that you seek and that you have the required financial backing, with or without a loan, the time comes to start work. However, before that it pays to stop for a moment and consider 'Image'.

Every business creates an impression on the world about it – sometimes intentionally and sometimes by accident. Once this image has registered in someone's mind (probably sub-consciously) it is very difficult to change it. This is why large companies spend vast amounts of money in creating a new image when they feel that it is commercially necessary. Usually this is because they have decided the time has come when the old 'We are a traditional company that you can trust' image must be replaced by a 'We are an up-to-date company, streamlined and efficient' image in order to compete with newcomers into their business who are taking away part of the market share by using a slick, modern image.

There are plenty of examples to choose from and so we can be fairly certain that it is important.

Now, the question is, 'What sort of image do I want to project?', and the answer will depend almost entirely on the target markets that you have selected and whether you are thinking of running a one man band, a professional partnership or a larger concern trading as a limited company.

The way Jane gets her staff to dress will affect her image.

I know a café somewhat like the one that Jane proposes to

open. There the staff wear long Victorian printed dresses coloured mainly pink and green, a style which is reflected throughout. The decor is generally pink and green, the napkins are pink, etc. This creates a particular atmosphere in which a certain group of customers feel very happy.

A hundred miles away is a very different establishment, where the staff wear white shirts with black bow ties and long white aprons over black trousers or skirts. The image has moved forward from Victorian times to the Edwardian era.

Any strong image will create an atmosphere that appeals to some but not to others. If it appeals to enough customers to provide the level of business required, then it has achieved what it set out to do. Those who don't like it do not matter. In such establishments, a low-key nondescript image which appeals to few and offends none may possibly work – but generally does not.

This type of image creation applies to any business, not just those who provide hospitality. The style of the letterhead, the logo used (if any – and that says something, too), the business cards, the signwriting on the shop or vehicle, the board a builder puts up outside a house when he is working on it, the way a shop displays its goods: these and many other factors all make up image.

Since image is all about selling, your target market should dictate the type of image that you will try to create. Make your image look too cheap and you will find that people will not have sufficient confidence in you. Make it look too glossy and the reaction may well be that you are going to prove too expensive.

Whether or not you employ a logo is really a matter of choice. They are used because they provide a useful form of shorthand: you see the logo and immediately know who is involved. If, for example, you are a craftsman and will be working in people's home for periods long enough to fix a board outside telling passers by who you are and what you are doing, a logo may be worth considering as some of those passers by will be driving past and will have no time to read anything but could identify a logo. However, for this to have any great value your logo needs to be well-known. That should not stop you using one: use is the only way that it can become well-known – but there is little point if there are not going to be enough opportunities to display it for it to become familiar. These opportunities exist when advertising in newspapers and it is not surprising that most estate agents use some form of logo (often incorporating the name) as it is displayed not only when they advertise but also outside the houses they are trying to sell. The average craftsman cannot hope for that level of exposure.

Some printers offer standard 'trade logos', such as a man carrying a hod of bricks. Whilst accepting that these immediately indicate the trade involved, they tend to make stationery look cheap and, in my opinion, offer little in return – if you want people to know what you do, there are better ways of doing it.

Whatever basic design you decide on, use it for everything. Design, in this case, includes layout, relative print size (size of name against address, etc.) and, of course, typeface. All your paperwork should match, as should any signwriting used on vehicles, shop fronts, menus, display boards, brochures, etc.

Unless you want something very avant garde and/or complicated, your local printer will be able to help create this design. The next level of help comes from graphic artists but using them adds to costs – which would be difficult to justify in most cases.

Printed Stationery

Letterheads
I know a number of tradesmen who have nothing more than a duplicate book in which they write everything – letters to potential customers, invoices, etc. – and they don't even have a rubber stamp with which to head the pages.

This may be satisfactory if you are a skilled craftsman who has no difficulty in getting more than enough work but it is a luxury that few can afford and not something I would recommend.

The absolute minimum, in my view, is a properly printed letterhead. This enables you to write (using a typewriter or word processing program – see Chapter 16) to potential customers, to suppliers, to your bank, etc., in a way that demonstrates that you are running a proper business and should be taken seriously. It makes sense to have your letterheads printed on A4 paper as that is the almost universal standard and this is not an area where it pays to be different.

Business Cards

In most businesses, you will want a business card to give to people to remind them how to contact you. However, before you order them from your friendly printer, do be sure that you will use them and remember that most cards hit the wastepaper basket within a very short space of time. If you are cold calling, you need something with which to introduce yourself and a business card is a near essential. If you only meet after making an appointment which you confirm in writing, there is little value in giving your contacts a card; they already know all it would tell them from your letter. If you only need a few cards, they can be obtained cheaply from machines usually found in shopping malls and motorway service areas.

Invoices

What sort you need will depend on the type of business. Letterheads can be used – invoices on letterheads should be typed and not written. In some cases such as a café or restaurant, all that is required is a receipt whilst in others a duplicate pad is sufficient. In both cases either these should be printed or you should invest in a rubber stamp so as to make the receipt or invoice 'official'. Proper invoice sets, with ruled lines if you want to write them out, are usually the third printed item that the new business acquires.

With Compliments slips

If you often send 'enclosures' which really do not need a covering letter, a 'With Compliments' slip is useful. These are usually the same width as the letterhead but only one third as deep. The main virtue of these slips is that you don't have to write an unnecessary letter – not to save money on printing.

Other

Most of the other items you see are not really essential. You can get away with using either a letterhead or a simple duplicate book (with a rubber stamp) in nearly all cases. If you decide to invest in a computer (see Chapter 16) you will be able to create most of the paperwork you want at little or no cost.

Printed Sales Literature

It is through your brochures, leaflets and price lists that you will project yourself, your image and your business most strongly.

If your intended customers are ordinary folk living in ordinary housing estates, avoid the temptation to make the literature too glossy. As we have seen, this can lead people to believe that they will find you too expensive. If, on the other hand, your customer is up-market, your literature will need to be up-market too. The same comments apply if you are intending to sell to other businesses.

Being Remembered

If at all possible you want something which will be seen time and time again so that your contacts and customers remember your name. There are three ways in which this can be achieved.

Businesses which deal in technical supplies and services which they sell to other businesses can provide their contacts with reference data covering information they frequently require. This data may be of a general nature or it may be specific to a given trade. An example could well be the engineer we met in Chapter 2 who decided to set up as a selling agent. If he obtained an agency for a firm who sold bearings, he would be able to offer his contacts a 'Bearing Equivalent' book so that they could compare the part numbers for several manufacturers. This agent should be able to obtain these from the manufacturer he represents as they probably publish one. Fixing a suitable sticky label to this reference book will mean it will act as a constant reminder. However, there is no guarantee that his reference book will be used –

after all, most bearing manufacturers produce something similar. If, as in this case, the books have cost the agent nothing (apart from the label), this doesn't really matter. It would have been a different matter if he had had to pay for them himself. Then considerable thought would have been needed to make the exercise worthwhile as he would have needed to produce something uniquely useful. This could be something which offers data that no one else has produced or it could be something which is better than anything available so that it is more likely to be used.

The second option has already been mentioned. Whenever possible, sticky labels should be fixed to equipment which has been supplied, serviced or repaired so that your name is noted (consciously or subconsciously) every time the equipment is used. Incidentally, our coal merchant put a laminated notice in our coal shed. Since it was there when we arrived, we naturally contacted him when we wanted to order fuel.

The third option is to provide contacts with personalised diaries, desk blotters, road maps, desk toys, etc. Whether or not these have any real effect almost certainly depends on the sort of business you are running. If the business does not attract repeat business (such as one which builds conservatories), personalised gifts are unlikely to be effective but if it relies on a regular stream of orders from a limited number of customers then they could well be worthwhile – especially if there is a good deal of competition.

14

STAFF

Introduction

Staff costs can, and often do, account for as much as 75 per cent of the gross profit of a small business. It follows that it is important that staff are all cost effective.

This means that they need to be efficient in their own jobs and operate as a team. To create this combination calls for careful selection and training. Training is needed to ensure that all know what the team as a whole is trying to achieve, what is required of them, what is required of any staff reporting to them and how they (and their staff) relate to other team members.

Without training, which need not be particularly formal, the potential of many staff members is never achieved, which means reduced profits for the business and reduced prospects for the staff.

Selecting Staff

There are a number of areas where everyone is an expert – and nobody knows anything about the subject. Initially this was said about education but I believe it is equally true when it comes to the matter of selecting staff. Everyone believes that they know how to go about it and that their interview techniques are as good as any. In fact, it is a highly complex subject and not even those working in employment agencies seem to have all the answers.

In Chapter 2 we looked at some of the problems associated with selecting candidates for selling posts. The same techniques can be applied to other areas.

When it comes to small businesses, there are three points to bear in mind: job description, presentation and compatibility.

Job Description

In a large organisation, the work for which a person is being enrolled can be defined within reasonably close limits. This is because there is enough work overall for each person to be responsible for a small portion of the workload. This is not true in small businesses where everyone may well be expected to lend a hand with just about anything.

Although it is difficult, it is vital that you, the employer, know exactly what duties you expect of people before you even think of starting to look for them. If you want them to be able to assist as required, write down all the various jobs you might want them to do. It may be a long list – that doesn't matter. What is important is that the prospective employees know what you want so that they can decide whether or not they are prepared to do it. On your side, you will have a clearer idea of the sort of people you need.

It is often too late when, a few weeks in, you ask someone to do something and he responds 'That's not what you employed me to do' and refuses to do it. This may sound far-fetched but I came across an example not that long ago. An assistant was wanted in a timber yard which, although primarily involved in wholesale business, had a small retail section. He was expected to be able to drive a forklift truck, handle an overhead crane, make fast loads on lorries and trailers, etc. What he had not been told was that he would be expected to serve in the retail section on certain Saturday mornings. What the employer did not know (because the subject did not arise) was that the employee was dyslexic and especially so when it came to numbers. In a previous job, mistakes on the till had resulted in his being accused of theft. Although the accusation was dropped when the circumstances became known, he had sworn he would never handle till transactions again. He refused to work on the retail counter and was sacked but was able to claim, and received, compensation for unfair dismissal. In this case the blame was entirely with the employer.

Presentation
In any small firm, the chances are that every employee at some stage will be in contact with customers. When that happens, the employee *is* the business as far as the customer is concerned.

It follows that all employees should present themselves in a way that does credit to the business.

Compatibility
A small business is like a family – it functions well only when everyone is getting on. As a bare minimum requirement, the employer should like the employees. If the employees also like the employer, many of the problems that can arise will be resolved before they become important.

Honesty
One of the nightmares associated with becoming an employer is the fear that one of the employees will prove to be less that honest. Obviously it is impossible to ensure that all persons employed will prove to be totally trustworthy but you can and should take references before you employ anyone.

Equally important is the need to reduce temptation as much as possible. If no records are kept and cash lives in an old tobacco tin or valuable stock is left lying around and everyone knows that the stock records are out of date, then you are almost asking one of your staff to take advantage.

Any cash handled should be properly accounted for – either by using a proper till or by making out duplicate pre-numbered receipts.

Stock, especially stock such as wines and spirits, must be controlled. A friend of mine runs a restaurant. Whenever a bottle of wine is opened, the cork is put in a container beside the till. Every night, the number of bottles in the 'cellar' plus the number of corks should equal last night's stock plus any additions. If it doesn't, there is an immediate enquiry to find out why not. He reckons he is 'saving' at least three bottles a week as a result of this simple control mechanism.

Staff Training

Obviously the amount of training required will vary enormously. Jane will be taking on kitchen and waiting staff. Probably all of them will have been in similar jobs before. Even so, there is benefit in training so as to weld them into a team that functions well even when the café is at its busiest.

In this case, the way in which the waiting staff write down the orders will have an effect on those in the kitchen. The way the kitchen staff put out the food will have an effect on those waiting at table. Time should be spent making sure that everyone understands not just the basics of their job but the ways in which they can become part of the team and the team can become more effective.

Training can take place at formal sessions or can be far less rigid. In Jane's case she might well decide that, after some formal sessions at the beginning, 'training' will take place at the end of the day when something has gone wrong. This may well involve the staff in making suggestions as to how mistakes can be put right and it is doubtful whether anybody would look upon it as a 'training session'. Nevertheless, that is what it would be.

If you are thinking of taking on any young people under one of the government training schemes, this part of life becomes more important. There are two tendencies that should be avoided. One is to treat the young people as cheap labour and make no real attempt at training. This is bad for both the business and the youngster – the business because it is not able to utilise the youngster properly and the youngster for obvious reasons. The second is to expect other workers, with no training skills or talents, to explain matters as they go along. Given the right person, this can be an ideal way of training the young but it really does depend on the skill and patience of the trainer and can result in the young person learning no more than unwanted bad habits and working practices. It is far better to pre-plan the training schedule and to formalise it to ensure that the youngster is trained in the right order by the right people.

Staff Incentives

In *Creating Sales Team Excellence,* the idea that financial rewards are the best incentive for salespeople is challenged. It is suggested that personal satisfaction can often be a greater incentive.

Certainly I have proved that a 'company bonus scheme' whereby all employees are paid a bonus if the company as a whole is doing well has no effect on personal performance. Even in the sales department, where commissions can be related to orders taken, the effect may not be as expected. One representative may well be working very hard trying to open up new contacts whilst another is coasting along on his existing customer bank. The latter may well be earning more – and, to be fair, earning more for the company in the short run – but the former may be of greater value to the company in the long run. Even if, when his work starts to pay off, he will then get his just rewards, he may become dispirited if he feels that what he is doing is failing to be properly recognised – with the result that pay day never arrives.

There are three 'incentives' that cost little and really do work. The first is 'consultation' – just asking the staff for their views and ideas. This makes them realise that they are important within the organisation and increases their 'personal satisfaction'. The second is gratitude – saying thank you when someone does something well or puts in extra effort. The third is trust – not just within the company but to the outside world. When I was a young man I worked for a company where every letter had to be signed by one of the directors. Then I moved and found that I was expected to sign my own post. The result was that I took a lot more trouble to ensure that what I wrote was right. There are many ways in which an employer can demonstrate trust and they are all worth using. Remember, if you can't trust your employees you shouldn't be employing them and if you can trust them you should let them know that you do.

Contract of Employment
Whenever you employ a person, a contract of employment, which clearly states the terms of the employment, must be drawn up and a copy handed to the employee. This is an area where legislation is often changed and so the exact requirements are likely to vary. There was a time when a number of firms provided blank forms which, if correctly completed,

complied with the law but these are no longer available. The sample Statement of Particulars of Employment is acceptable at the moment but may not be so in the future.

You will see that in that sample there is no reference to any pension arrangements. This is because – unless you employ enough staff to be required by law to offer stakeholder pensions (and remember this is a part of employment law that is being changed quite often) – you are most unlikely to include any special arrangements in the early days of the business and any such arrangements that you make later on would be noted in a separate statement.

Each employee must have a job title which should convey the nature of the work. However, an employee may well be asked to carry out duties not suggested by the title. Thus Jane's 'waiting staff' may well be asked to help to clean the café or even to assist the kitchen staff on occasions.

If you sack an employee who has worked for you for more than three months, (s)he is entitled to a redundancy payment. That is straightforward enough under most circumstances. However, if you are thinking about buying a business which has employees already and you want to retain those employees then the position is rather different. So long as you agree to take on the existing employees under the same (or better) conditions of employment, they are not entitled to any redundancy pay as they have not lost their jobs. However, if you change your mind a few weeks or even months later the amount of redundancy pay due to the employee would depend not on the length of service with you but the length of service from the date they commenced working in the job. Clearly, if the person selling you the business has to find redundancy pay, the chances are that the price you will have to pay for the business will be that much higher. That means it could be to your advantage to take on the staff, unless there is a good reason not to. On the other hand, when you buy is the time to decide who you want and who you don't – leaving it until later can cause problems with other members of staff.

This explains the use of the phrase 'and employment with your previous employer does not count as part of your continuous period of employment'. If you are taking over

STATEMENT OF PARTICULARS OF EMPLOYMENT	
Employer's Name and Address	*Enter the full name and address of the business. If you are using a trading name the form is 'E Jones trading as Jones Plumbing'.*
Employee's Name and Address	*Enter the full name and address of the employee.*

The following are particulars of your employment as at *enter the full date.*

Your place of work is *enter the full address of the premises on which or from which the employee works.*

Your employment began on *enter the full date* and employment with your previous employer does not count as part of your continuous period of employment.

Terms and Conditions	
Job Title	*Enter the employee's job title.* Your job title conveys the nature of the work you are required to perform but you will be required from time to time to carry out such other duties as may reasonably be required.
Remuneration	*Enter the employee's pay details including all overtime, commission and bonus payments.* Remuneration is paid by cash/cheque/by transfer to a specified bank or building society account. *Modify this clause as required.* Weekly wages are paid on Friday mornings/ Monthly salaries are paid on the last working day in each calendar month. *Use whichever clause applies.* Commission payments cover all sales made to the *date* day of each calendar month. *Use this clause only if it applies, modifying as required.*

Hours of Work	*Insert the normal hours of work.*
Holidays and Holiday Pay	You are entitled to *insert the number of* days' paid holiday per annum. The holiday year is for the 12 months commencing *enter the date – generally but not always 1st April.*
	In addition to the holiday entitlement stated above, you are entitled to all public holidays with pay. If the interests of the business require it, you may be called upon to work on such public holidays in which event substitute days will be allocated or a payment in lieu given at an agreed holiday rate.
	Holidays must be taken in the holiday year.
	Should your employment come to an end before all accrued holiday is taken, you will receive payment in lieu. If you have taken more holiday than has accrued, your final payment will be reduced by the amount involved.
Sickness and Injury	You will receive full pay for absence where that absence does not exceed *enter number of days (usually three)* days at any one time or *enter number of days (usually fifteen)* days in any one calendar year subject to sickness or injury being reported at once. If you are absent for more than *enter the same as above (e.g. three)* days you must send a note from your doctor certifying your incapacity to work. Payments for longer periods would not be less than the amount provided by any law for the time being in force.
Rights to Notice	You are entitled to receive *enter amount* notice. You are obliged to give *enter amount* notice.

Disciplinary Rules and Procedures	Details of Disciplinary Rules and Procedures will be found in the attached Employment Code of Practice.
Grievance Procedures	Details of Grievance Procedures will be found in the attached Employment Code of Practice.

Should any of the above particulars change, the employer shall provide not later than one month after the change a written statement containing particulars of the change.

Signed for and on behalf of the employer:

Date

Signed by the employee:

Date

staff when buying a business, the word 'not' is deleted from that phrase.

Discipline and Grievances
All members of staff must know how to find the name of the senior member of staff who can be approached if a staff member has a grievance and to whom a disciplinary matter would be referred. Although that may cover the employer as far as the law is concerned, it means that it can be very difficult to sack an employee, especially on the spot, regardless of what the employee may have done.

In order to protect both the employer and the employee, an Employment Code of Practice should be drawn up and a copy given to each member of staff. The example shown is obviously generalised and would need to be modified in many cases. Nevertheless, it contains the main points to take into consideration.

EMPLOYMENT CODE OF PRACTICE

1.   *Introduction*

1.1   *This document gives practical guidance on both Disciplinary Rules and Procedures and Grievance Rules and Procedures. Its aim is to help both the company and employees.*

1.2   *Disciplinary Rules and Procedures are necessary for promoting fairness and order in the treatment of individuals and in the conduct of industrial relations. They also assist an organisation to operate effectively. Rules set standards of conduct at work; procedure helps to ensure that the standards are adhered to and also provide a fair method of dealing with alleged failures to observe them.*

1.3   *It is important that employees know what standards are expected of them and the Contracts of Employment Act 1972 (as amended by the Employment Pro-*

tection Act 1975) requires employers to provide written information for their employees about certain aspects of their disciplinary rules and procedures.

1.4   *This document is intended to ensure that all employees are aware of the likely consequence of breaking rules and in particular the type of conduct which may warrant summary dismissal.*

2.   Disciplinary Rules and Procedures

2.1   *The disciplinary procedure is not intended primarily as a means of imposing sanctions but rather to encourage improvements in conduct.*

2.2   *Disciplinary procedures will:*

(a)   *Be in writing to the employee concerned.*

(b)   *Provide for matters to be dealt with quickly.*

(c)   *Indicate the disciplinary action(s) that may be taken.*

(d)   *Provide for the individual concerned to be fully informed as to the complaint against him/her and be given an opportunity to state his/her case before decisions are reached.*

(e)   *Ensure that, except as specified below, no employee is dismissed for the first breach of discipline.*

(f)   *Ensure that disciplinary action is not taken until the case has been fully investigated.*

(g)   *Ensure that the individual concerned is given an explanation for any penalty that may be imposed.*

      (h)   *Provide a right of appeal and specify the appeal procedure.*

2.3   *When a disciplinary matter arises, the supervisor or manager should establish the facts promptly before recollections fade by taking, in writing, statements from any available witnesses.*

2.4   *In serious cases not warranting summary dismissal, consideration would be given to the suspension of the individual concerned pending a full investigation. This suspension would be with pay.*

2.5   *Before any decision is made, the individual would be interviewed and given the opportunity to state his/her case.*

2.6   *Often supervisors will give informal oral warnings for the purpose of improving conduct when employees commit minor infringements of the established standards of conduct. However, where the facts of the case appear to call for disciplinary action, other than summary dismissal, the following procedure should normally be observed:*

      (a)   *In the case of minor offences the individual should be given a formal oral warning or, if the issue is more serious, there should be a written warning setting out the nature of the offence and the likely consequence of further offences. In either case, the individual should be advised that the warning constitutes the first formal stage of procedure.*

      (b)   *Further misconduct might warrant a final written warning which should contain a statement that any recurrence would lead to suspension, dismissal or some other penalty as the case may be.*

(c)   The final step might be disciplinary suspension without pay, or dismissal.

2.7   Except in the event of an oral warning, details of any disciplinary action should be given in writing to the employee and the employee should be told of any right of appeal, how to appeal and to whom to appeal.

2.8   When determining the disciplinary action to be taken, account should be taken of the employee's record and all other relevant factors and such action should satisfy the test of reasonableness.

2.9   Special consideration should be given to the way in which disciplinary procedures are to operate in exceptional cases. For example:

(a)   Employees to whom the full procedure is not immediately available such as workers in isolated locations or where, for example, no one is present with the necessary authority to take disciplinary action.

(b)   Criminal offences outside employment should not be treated as automatic reasons for dismissal regardless of whether the offence has any relevance to the duties of the individual as an employee. The main consideration should be whether or not the offence is one that makes the individual unsuitable for his/her type of work and/or unacceptable to other employees. Employees should not be dismissed solely because a charge against them is pending or because they are absent through having been held in custody.

2.10   The following offences are likely to attract summary dismissal:

(a) *The removal of any property belonging to the company or to any customer of the company or to any individual employed by the company without prior permission of the owner.*

(b) *Any breach of confidentiality likely to result in damage to the company's reputation.*

(c) *Any absence from the place of work of more than seven days unless through sickness or injury as specified in the Terms and Conditions in the Statement of Particulars of Employment or with prior permission.*

(d) *Any physical assault on any person within working hours or on property owned by or rented to the company.*

(e) *Any deliberate action likely to cause damage to any property rented to the company, any property owned by the company, any property owned by customers of the company or any property owned by any other individual employed by the company.*

2.11 *The following offences are likely to attract disciplinary action other than summary dismissal.*

(a) *Persistent poor time-keeping.*

(b) *Persistent failure properly to carry out the duties and responsibilities required of any employee.*

2.12 *Appeals: Appeals against disciplinary action should be addressed to . . . . . . These should be in writing wherever possible.*

2.13 *Independent Arbitration is sometimes a means of resolving disciplinary issues. Where the parties concerned agree, it may become the final stage of procedure.*

2.14 *Records shall be kept detailing the nature of any breach of disciplinary rules, the action taken and the reasons for it, whether an appeal was lodged, its outcome and any subsequent development. Such records will be carefully safeguarded and kept confidential.*

2.15 *Under normal circumstances breach of disciplinary rules shall be disregarded after six months of satisfactory service.*

3. **Grievances**

3.1 *In the event that an employee has a grievance, the grievance should be addressed to . . . . . ., preferably in writing.*

3.2 *It is important that an employee having a grievance related to his/her employment should bring it to the attention of the above person at the earliest possible opportunity. This is true whether the matter is personal to an individual or is a matter which affects others as well.*

3.3 *The proper use of this procedure will not prejudice an employee's employment in any way.*

This may seem over complicated for an employer with, say, only one employee. Any employer who has had to face a claim for unfair dismissal would confirm that it is only sensible. What at the time seems like a clear-cut breach of common sense employment law, well deserving summary dismissal, can look very different in a court of law. In any event, a few sheets of paper are far cheaper than even the least costly compensation claim.

PAYE and the Inland Revenue

As soon as you become an employer, you must register with the Inland Revenue and administer the Pay As You Earn scheme.

Many small businesses try to avoid becoming involved and claim that their 'employees' are actually self-employed and responsible for their own tax. It is worth checking with the Inland Revenue if you have any doubts, simply because, at the end of the day, if the Inland Revenue rule that the person *was* an employee, it will be *you* who is responsible for any tax due and not the employee. To make matters worse, they will judge that the money you paid was net and not gross. So, if you decided to pay someone £160 per week and two years later the Inland Revenue issued you with a demand, they would assume that the gross pay was in the order of £213 per week and issue you with a demand for something in the order of £5,500 (the exact figures would depend on the ruling tax rates). In addition, you would have to pay both the employer's and employee's National Insurance contributions. Although it creates paperwork, it really is essential to employ people on a proper basis.

Health and Safety at Work

It is the employer's responsibility to meet the Health and Safety at Work legislation requirements and to ensure that all employees are aware of the action required following fire, accident, etc.

Most of the requirements of this legislation are common sense and staff notification can be achieved by putting up notices. A variety of standard notices are available and it is usually only a case of choosing the ones that apply to the business.

Employer's Liability

As soon as you have employees (official or otherwise) you are required to insure against claims which they may make against you. This is usually a part of a 'Combined Insurance Policy' which covers all the main insurable requirements of a business.

Most reputable insurance companies provide suitable cover – with a variety of policies being available depending on the business.

Finally ...
The law on employment often changes and that has become even more true now that many aspects of employment are covered by both UK and European legislation. It is the employer's responsibility to be aware of any changes that affect the situation.

Many trade associations keep a watching brief on behalf of their members and send out details of any relevant changes. There are a number of reasons why you may decide to join the association covering your business and advice on employment matters may be only one.

Another gateway to advice on all aspects of employment law is your local Employment Service Job Centre. That may sound incredible but they should be able to provide you with leaflets covering all you need to know and, in addition, although they may not be able to give you advice themselves, they are able to make arrangements for you to contact whatever specialist adviser you may need.

An invaluable source of 'impartial advice' when things go wrong is the Advisory, Conciliation and Arbitration Service. They can be contacted through one of their regional offices or at their London office.

15

ODDS AND ENDS

The Law and Businesses

As soon as you open a business, whether it be from home or more formal business premises, you will need to comply with various rules and regulations.

The problem is that these tend to change quite frequently and so the only sensible approach is to point you in the right direction to find advice.

Insurance

If your business can in any way damage other people or property you need an insurance policy to cover those risks. This is no different from third party car insurance. The best source of advice is a reputable insurance company. It is in their interests to be up to date and to know what they are talking about. Even so, since the source of advice is free, it is always sensible to approach more than one office so that you can benefit from a 'second opinion' – quite apart from the fact that shopping around could well reduce the premium.

Obviously, insurance companies want to sell insurance. Be sure that only those risks which really need to be covered are covered.

Contract Law

Contract Law is extremely complicated. It covers any agreement between two or more parties. As far as the average business is concerned, the areas which are most likely to crop up are leases and contracts with customers/suppliers.

There is a great temptation to ignore the potential dangers of contract law and, fortunately, most of the time most of us get away with it. However, only a few weeks ago a client of mine discovered that an agreement that he had been using for years was faulty, with the result that he had no option but to write off an invoice of many hundreds of pounds.

There is no need to over-react, though. If your average order is small in value, detailed terms and conditions are probably unnecessary and the cost of having them drafted, checked by a solicitor and printed on your stationery has to be borne in mind. However, if you are likely to be carrying out a limited number of high value jobs or you are working in an area where disputes frequently occur, some thought should be given to this problem.

The best source of advice is a solicitor who specialises in commercial law. He will be able to advise you as to what you need to do and when you need to do it. Remember, if the first your customer knows of your trading terms is when the invoice arrives, he may find them unacceptable, refuse to take the goods on that basis and leave you with a problem.

Tax Law
There are three sources of advice: HM Inland Revenue, HM Customs and Excise and, of course, an accountant.

It may come as a surprise to find that the tax inspectors at the Inland Revenue are often the best advisers when it comes to income tax, PAYE, etc. Subject only to their being sure that the enquirer is telling the truth, the whole truth and nothing but the truth, my experience is that they will bend over backwards to help the taxpayer, whether it is a matter of complying with regulations or trying to sort out how much tax is payable.

Customs and Excise, in their role as VATmen, are equally helpful when it comes to sorting out matters of principle if less so in assisting with actual figures.

In both cases, since you are dealing with the horse's mouth, you can rely on what they say. The same should be true (and generally is) if you consult an accountant. The main difference is that you will have to pay the accountant – but then you will not have to deal with the officials yourself.

Company Law
This is another complex subject but it only applies if you are
running a limited liability company. For a start you will need
to employ a Chartered Accountant as Auditor. The accountant
that you use can also handle all the matters which are the duty
of the Company Secretary or, if you prefer, act as a mentor to
the person appointed.

Although the accountant may not be able to advise on all
matters pertaining to company law, a good one will know
when to tell you to go and see a specialist solicitor. However,
it is your duty to comply with the law: if you are not sure that
the accountant is giving you good advice, go and see a
solicitor who specialises in this subject.

Grants and Government Sponsored Loan Schemes
The position varies widely from one part of the country to
another and there are many possible sources of assistance. The
only sure way through the maze is through the Department of
Trade and Industry. They have local offices throughout the
country and will be able to tell you what is available in your
area. Incidentally, their services cover much more than assisting in obtaining grants or loans supported by the Government
Loan Guarantee Scheme (which, in certain cases, enables
banks to make loans to people even though they do not have
the security normally required).

Just because you are eligible for a grant does not mean that
you will get it. Many are discretionary and the available funds
are limited.

An increasing number of local authorities are also becoming involved in grant aided projects. A call to your local
council may prove worthwhile but do not be over surprised if
your local authority cannot assist.

A word of caution: because the whole business of grant aid
is extremely complicated, a number of firms offer assistance
against a fee. Obviously I cannot comment on all of them, but
the ones I have come into contact with do no more than feed
details into a computer database and produce a list of possible
sources. They typically charge a fee for this service and expect
the enquirer to sign an agreement whereby they also receive a

percentage of any funds raised if raised from one of the organisations on their list. But all the sources of finance on their database will be known to one of the agencies that can be contacted through the DTI and they will provide the information free of charge.

Life Assurance and Pensions

Most people these days insure themselves so that any mortgage they have is paid off should they die or become permanently unfit for work. The same logic should apply to any loans taken out for business purposes and some lenders will only lend if there is life cover assigned to the lender (i.e. the lender receives the proceeds from the policy and not the policyholder). This offers the lender additional security and they have every right to demand it.

Because banks also run life assurance offices, they will press very hard for any new policy to be taken out through their affiliated life assurance company. This is perfectly reasonable. However, they are unlikely to insist that the policy is purchased through them if the customer would prefer to deal with another provider.

Basic life cover is called 'Term Assurance'. For an agreed term of years the insurance company will cover your life for a given amount against a given premium. There is no element of saving within the plan and, like ordinary insurance policies, you 'lose' the premiums if you do not make a claim during the life of the policy. These policies usually have a number of add-on features – they can be extended to cover permanent disability, the loss of a limb, etc. Most policies allow you to opt for 'premium waiver' which means that your premiums are paid for you during periods of temporary disability through illness or accident. Term assurance is the cheapest form of life assurance – but that does not mean it is always the right one to choose.

Next up the ladder is 'Whole of Life Assurance'. This is very similar to term assurance except that the policy remains in force until the death of the policyholder (subject, of course, to premiums being paid). Obviously this means that the policy will eventually pay out and that means higher premiums although the younger you are when the policy starts, the lower the premiums will be. It often comes as a surprise to find that 'Whole of Life' is not *that* much more expensive than 'Term' – in any event it is always worth checking the difference in cost.

The life assurance most people know about are those policies with savings plans attached – such as the 'Endowment' plans designed to run alongside mortgages. Because part of the premium is put to the savings plan, the premiums are far higher than those for the policies described above. Sadly, even with the tax advantages these policies attract, those savings plans do not always prove to be as profitable as people had hoped.

It is your decision whether you combine life cover with savings or opt for life cover alone and look after your savings yourself. Do remember that changing horses in midstream may not be a good idea – as we have seen, premiums are linked to age and starting something now with a view to changing it in a few years' time can be costly.

There is a great deal of temptation (aggravated by life assurance salespeople) to start a pension plan as soon as possible after embarking down the road of self-employment. It must not be forgotten that the tax advantages attached to pensions only apply if a profit is made and that the entitlement to put money into a pension plan also depends on that profit. To avoid future complication, no plan should be started unless you are as sure as you can be that the profits you project will be achieved. If you are running a limited liability company, the rules are different and pensions are linked to directors' pay rather than profits (although the amount directors can pay themselves out of the company is linked to profits and so the same comments apply).

This leads onto the best source for life assurance and pensions. That is a very difficult decision for the average layman and is important to businesspeople who should be looking in all areas to buy as prudently as possible, balancing what they buy against the cost. In the early years of a business it is usually sensible to try to cover any personal insurance requirements as cheaply as possible and, as with other forms of insurance, that means shopping around. In the end, the best possible source is probably a life assurance salesperson (whether he or she is a representative tied to one company or an independent insurance broker) who understands your position and in whom you have absolute trust. It is worth remembering that even independent brokers who seem to have a wide range of companies in their portfolios will only be acting for a handful of life companies. The average broker holds eight or so agencies out of well over a hundred companies. This means that even after receiving a quotation from an independent broker, you might find a better deal by going to see someone else.

16

COMPUTERS

If you already own a computer and are very happy working with it, you will no doubt want to use it for your new business and this chapter is not really for you. If, however, you are one of those who knows nothing about them, please read on.

The fact is that anyone starting a business today will – almost certainly and no matter how reluctantly – find himself using a computer at some point. Obviously, since businesses were being run before computers were invented, a computer is not essential. However, you could say the same things about many other tools. How many carpenters these days would consider working without at least some powered equipment?

If you don't worry about how it actually works, there is nothing magical about a computer. It is simply a tool which has the capability of doing certain things very well indeed. In some ways it can be compared to a car – you don't need to know how it works to drive it but you do need to know that the better a driver you are, the better the car will perform. A computer is just like that.

More to the point, modern equipment enables unskilled people to carry out tasks they would otherwise have to leave to others. Being no craftsman, I am incapable of sawing a piece of wood so that it ends up true if I use a normal handsaw but I make a fairly good job of it when I use a power saw which guarantees the blade stays at right angles to the wood being cut.

Forget all the mystique associated with computers – if

children of five and six can make sense of them, so can anyone thinking about starting a business. The point is that the children are not frightened of them or of damaging them (partly, no doubt, because they have not paid for them) and that means they are always happy to hit the keys just to see what happens which is basically exactly the right way to learn.

Having said that, it would be silly to suggest that all you need to do is to buy a computer and away you go. For a start, you have to decide what you need to buy and that can prove to be very complicated indeed. The two most common sorts of computer are – PCs and Apple Macs. The following all applies to the PC as that format has a far greater range of programs available and is most generally used. Apple Macs are superb if you are involved in computer-aided design and other creative activities – but if you are, you will know that already.

As an experiment, I telephoned a number of computer suppliers and – pretending to be Jane's husband – asked the same question of them all:

'I am about to start a business with my wife, nothing complicated – just a tea room. We think we should be using a computer but we know nothing about them. What would you advise we bought?'

The replies were very interesting.

Case 1:
'You will have to speak to one of our salespeople but they are all busy at the moment. Please give me your telephone number and I'll ask one of them to call you back.'

This could, of course, have been the truth but I telephoned that company eight times at various times of day from very first thing to just two minutes before they closed and I always received exactly the same reply. Now, I had withheld my telephone number quite deliberately as I did not want to be pestered by calls – that would have been true had my enquiry been genuine – and I came to the conclusion that they really wanted that telephone number before they would give advice. I recount the story for what it is worth.

Case 2:
'You don't need anything over the top. Have you a budget figure in mind?'

'No, but obviously I don't want to spend more than I have to.'

'In that case I would suggest a fairly fast processor with 64 meg of RAM – you need that for multi-tasking and 64 should be OK but 120 would be better – and 20 gig of hard disk which should be ample. Computer, printer, CD writer and scanner – that's for putting pictures onto presentation – and Microsoft Works to give you word processing, spreadsheet and a database'.

'And what about the accounts?' I asked.

'Well, you could buy a package called Sage but that's a bit over the top and you can keep simple accounts on the spreadsheet.'

'Right. Do you supply training?'

'We don't but you can get training at adult training centres who do evening classes but I shouldn't bother. It's easy enough to pick up as you go along.'

'Oh, good.'

Now, you will remember that I had said I knew nothing about computers, so clearly the above was really incomprehensible to me. It would be churlish to blame the young man I spoke to. He came over very well but opted for a specification well in advance of the basic – but nowhere near the top-of-the-range. We will look in detail at his 'specification' in a minute.

Case 3:
This was disgraceful. I was offered a top of the range package with a whole range of software for a substantial amount of money. This is the sort of thing you will see offered in the newspapers and has almost nothing to do with business requirements.

Case 4:
'All you need to start with is the most basic computer and printer that we can offer. As far as programs are concerned,

*there's probably somewhere near you offering courses and
really the best thing would be to go along and learn the basics
before you buy anything. Find out what's on the market and
what you want.'*

This is pretty good advice – and, perhaps surprisingly, it came
from a well-known chain store.

Case 5:
'Don't buy a computer – you don't need one.'

That last was very refreshing. In this instance I was talking to
a specialist firm who make bespoke computers for businesses
of all sizes. When I pressed, I was told that a cash business of
that sort could manage very well with a simple handwritten
cash book and you could get other people to produce menus,
etc., at a fraction of the cost.

So just what should we buy?

All computers operate around a Central Processing Unit
(sometimes called the CPU and sometimes simply the 'processor'). The 'speed' of the CPU determines how quickly the
computer works. All modern CPUs are fast – far faster than you
are likely to need, unless you are planning a business specifically
designed to make use of modern computer technology in which
case the odds are you will not be reading this chapter.

Computers have three ways of storing information. The first
is called ROM which stands for Read Only Memory. Here the
computer stores all the basic instructions which are installed
when the computer is built. Generally speaking, the information embedded in the ROM cannot be changed and it remains
intact when the power to the computer is switched off. The
second storage is called RAM which stands for Random
Access Memory. This is a short-term storage facility as everything contained within it is lost the moment the computer is
shut down. Information can be stored in RAM and extracted
from RAM very quickly. Lastly, there are the physical units
where information can be stored on a permanent basis but both
storage and extraction take time. During normal operation, the
physical unit used is called the 'hard disk'. This stores the

information magnetically and is built into the computer. Hard disks can carry a tremendous amount of information. When the computer is operating, it stores as much as possible in the RAM which 'trades' information with the hard disk as necessary.

Thus the more RAM available, the faster the computer works. Having said that, most business requirements operate quite happily on 16 megabytes. However, to be fair to the salesman in Case 2 he did mention 'multi-tasking' as the reason for so much RAM. This is where you ask the computer to carry out more than one job at the same time – such as printing a long document while you access the Internet. Under those circumstances, the more RAM the better.

I was offered 20 gigabytes of hard disk. That is far more than you are likely to want. The computer on which this book is being written has a 2 gigabyte hard disk and I have never used more than half that capacity.

Obviously a printer is needed but I question the need for a CD writer or a scanner.

(Incidentally, it is almost certain that the figures quoted in Case 2 will be out of date by the time this revision is in print because the computer industry is extremely fast moving and so this specification will look very pedestrian in no time at all.)

Apart from the hard disk, there are a number of other ways of storing information and it is a very good idea to have your files duplicated – backed-up in computer speak – external to the computer so that in the event of a disaster you don't lose all your work.

The commonest way is to store files on a 'floppy disk' which is another magnetic storage system. The computer will have a 'disk drive' unit into which a floppy is put and files are then copied to it. The problem with floppy disks is that they have limited capacity, but even so it is likely to be enough for most requirements.

Then there are 'tapes' which can have very large capacity and which work in an external unit linked to the computer by a cable. These are commonly used to produce a daily back-up of everything stored on the computer's hard disk when using floppy disks is no longer practical.

You can install as an external unit a device called a 'Zip

Drive'. These use special zip disks with a capacity equivalent to from 100 to 175 conventional disks.

Lastly, there is the Compact Disc or CD. Most computers now carry a CD reader because most programs these days are supplied on CD. CDs have a very large capacity and, as with music CDs, they rarely fault and usually maintain high quality. If you want to make your own CDs you need a unit called a CD Writer. It can be built in, or combined in the CD drive. You are extremely unlikely to need one.

The same applies to the scanner. This is a unit which 'scans' images (pictures, etc.) and converts them into a digital format which can be read by the computer. Scanners are of value only if you need that facility.

To sum up: the advice given in Case 4 was right – you want the most basic unit that is available to you. There are times when a higher specification is useful. If you want to use the computer for games, the more powerful the computer (in terms of both CPU and RAM), the better the games will run. If you want to work with graphics, and especially with digital photographs, you may need more RAM and, if you want to store this sort of work, you will require a large hard disk.

So much for the 'hardware' – what about the programs (or 'software') that we shall need?

The Computer at Work

Why do we want a computer and what shall we be doing with it? Well, obviously we want a computer to do those tasks it does better than we can or quicker than we can. Jane wants to use her computer to write letters, to produce menus and publicity leaflets and to keep her books. She may also want to maintain a record of all the local businesses so as to be able to give or send them sales literature.

Writing Letters

Computers use word processing programs to produce documents. The word processor uses the same basic keyboard as an old fashioned typewriter with a few extra keys offering special facilities.

The main difference between a typewriter and a word processor is that what you type is displayed on a screen rather than on paper. This means that you can look at what you have written and change it before passing it to the printer to create the finished item. The ability to change things on screen before printing is a huge benefit. You can play with words until you are satisfied that they are actually saying what you mean to say. That is fairly important in general life but infinitely more so in business where what you write may well form part of a contract.

Another advantage is that you can store what you write in the computer's storage system and recall it whenever you want to. This can save a good deal of time if you need to write identical or similar letters to a number of people. The classic case is where people have failed to pay an account on time. Much the same letter is sent out to all, but the name, address, date and amount due obviously vary. If a dozen such letters need to be sent out each month, the computer will soon begin to pay for itself in time saved.

Producing Menus and Leaflets
When Jane decided to try to produce her menus on the computer using her word processor, she started by just typing it out and it looked like this:

General Menu served 10 am to 6.30 pm
Coffee: £1.00 per cup or £1.20 per mug
Tea: 85p per single person pot
Hot Chocolate: £1.10 per cup or £1.30 per mug
Biscuits (selection of six): £1.00
Buttered Toast: 30p per round
Toasted Teacakes: 50p each
Sandwiches – Beef, Ham or Cheese: £1.10
Sandwiches – Toasted: £1.40

Jane decided that she would like it to be in a script so she changed the 'font' to one called Brush Script. This was the result:

General Menu served 10 am to 6.30 pm
Coffee: £1.00 per cup or £1.20 per mug
Tea: 85p per single person pot
Hot Chocolate: £1.10 per cup or £1.30 per mug
Biscuits (selection of six): £1.00
Buttered Toast: 30p per round
Toasted Teacakes: 50p each
Sandwiches – Beef, Ham or Cheese: £1.10
Sandwiches –Toasted: £1.40

She decided that this is all right but might be a bit difficult for
some people to read so she decided to make it bigger. She felt
it would look better if it was in the middle of the page – or
'centered'.

General Menu served 10 am to 6.30 pm
Coffee: £1.00 per cup or £1.20 per mug
Tea: 85p per single person pot
Hot Chocolate: £1.10 per cup or £1.30 per mug
Biscuits (selection of six): £1.00
Buttered Toast: 30p per round
Toasted Teacakes: 50p each
Sandwiches – Beef, Ham or Cheese: £1.10
Sandwiches – Toasted: £1.40

She felt that looked a lot better but that the heading could be
bigger and bolder. This is the final result:

General Menu served 10 am to 6.30 pm

Coffee: £1.00 per cup or £1.20 per mug
Tea: 85p per single person pot
Hot Chocolate: £1.10 per cup or £1.30 per mug
Biscuits (selection of six): £1.00
Buttered Toast: 30p per round
Toasted Teacakes: 50p each
Sandwiches (Beef, Ham or Cheese): £1.10
Sandwiches (Toasted): £1.40

Changing 'fonts' (the style of printing), the size of the text, the 'form' of the text (it can be regular, **bold**, *italic*, underlined or a combination of those) and the position of the text can dramatically improve the appearance of any printed document.

You can buy special programs to produce leaflets, brochures and so on – called 'publishing programs' – and other programs to produce special artwork but, as you can see from the above, most modern word processing programs are so good that you may well find you can produce any publicity material you need without having to buy any other program.

Book-Keeping
You can keep books on a spreadsheet program or a special book-keeping program. First, we will look at how a spreadsheet works.

Essentially a spreadsheet is made up of cells arranged in columns and rows so that each cell can be readily identified by reference to the column heading (usually a letter or letters) and the row number. Here is what a small, blank spreadsheet looks like.

	A	B	C	D	E	F	G
1							
2							
3							
4							

Each cell has an alphanumeric identifier – in this case from A1 in the top left corner to G4 in the bottom right. Each cell can contain general information – such as a column heading in text – or numbers. When we use numbers, we can enter formula into certain cells so that any arithmetic we want is carried out automatically. Here is an example.

	A	B	C	D	E	F	G
1	Week Number	1	2	3	4	5	6
2	Sales	120	118	111	128	136	127
3	Direct Costs @ 35%	42	41	39	45	48	44
4	Gross Profit	78	77	72	83	88	83

The week numbers in cells B1 to G1 are not numbers but text (we do not want to carry out any calculations with them and if this had been a monthly spreadsheet the headings would have been 'Jan', 'Feb', etc.).

We have to enter our sales figures in cells B2 to G2.

We have put a formula in cells B3 to G3 which instructs as we work across, 'Multiply the figure in B2 by 0.35', 'Multiply the figure in C2 by 0.35', etc.

We have put a formula in cells B4 to G4 which instructs as we work across, 'Take the figure in B3 from the figure in B2', 'Take the figure in C3 from the figure in C2', etc.

When we put a formula into a cell it is not displayed. However, when we put figures into row 2, rows 3 and 4 are automatically calculated for us. The computer is not only quicker than we are, it will calculate without error. For this sort of work it is both better and faster. Incidentally, the actual formulae vary slightly from spreadsheet to spreadsheet but they are easily understood.

Using the above techniques Jane could create a cash book on the computer which would give her the same facilities as a normal cash book except it would carry out the arithmetic for her.

However, she might well decide that she wants to use a more sophisticated accounts program which makes it easier to reconcile her books with her bank account and to keep track of her ledgers. There is a wide variety from which she could choose but she would be wise to select the simplest capable of meeting her needs.

Incidentally, Jane could have used the spreadsheet for the

financial analysis in her Business Plan. Likewise, she could use them for her management accounts – comparing actual against budget – if she decides she needs them.

Keeping Records
To be honest, it is not likely, in Jane's particular business, that there would be enough benefit to make it worth keeping records of individual customers or prospects. However, that is not always true and there are many cases where keeping records of one sort or another is vital.

The programs used are known as 'databases'. The database is a card index. Most database programs enable the user to design the card they want – usually a very simple job – and can hold as many different card indexes as are required. Here is a very simple sales contact record.

Firm				
Address				
Address 2				
Town				
County				
Post Code				
Telephone			Fax	
Contact				
Last Call	By		On	
Last Order	On		Value	
Notes				

The data, or information, is typed into the blank areas – called fields – and these are designed to hold various types of information. In the above example, all of the fields except two would be 'text fields'. The exceptions are the two labelled 'On' (which are date fields) and the one labelled 'Value' (which is a numeric field). Numbers in such fields can be used in calculations. There are other field types but they are less common.

Where the database scores over the card index is the ease and speed with which you can find records. In the case above, it would be possible to 'search' the database to find a record using the name of the firm, the name of the contact, the telephone number or even the post code (although that could mean you were offered more than one record from which to choose).

In the case shown above, using a search on the 'Last Call On' field enables you to find records for sales contacts due to be called. I am sure you can think of other searches that would be of use. To extract this sort of information from a card index would take many hours.

Other Computer Options

Desktop Publishing

We have seen that Jane intends to use her word processor to create her publicity materials – but there will be those who need a much more sophisticated program because they want to produce more sophisticated leaflets, brochures, etc.

The Desktop Publisher goes some way towards meeting this requirement. It enables you to use diagrams, drawings, photographs, etc., and to create a wide range of special effects. It can take quite a long time to master a desktop publisher package and computer printing tends to be rather slow when producing complicated graphics.

Unless there are real savings to be made, you are probably better off leaving this sort of thing to the professionals while you make money doing whatever it is that you are doing – unless, of course, you just enjoy creating your own material and do it in your spare time.

The Contact Management Program

This is a specialist program that you may find useful. It combines various concepts in one program. The one I use is

basically a database into which details of all my contacts are
entered but this is a list of some of the other facilities.

Associated with each contact is a memo board on which
notes can be kept.

Associated with each contact is a word processor designed
to produce letters.

The program can sort my contacts into groups and print out
lists.

Because the computer is linked to the telephone line via a
modem, I can auto dial all contacts.

There is a calendar to record all appointments and things to
be done.

Any event on the calendar can create an 'alarm' if required.

Email
There is no doubt that the ability to use electronic mail (or
email for short) can, in certain circumstances, be invaluable.

The basic requirements are for you to install a device called
a 'modem' to link your computer to your telephone line and to
arrange email facilities with an appropriate supplier (called an
Internet Service Provider or ISP). You are then able to send
messages to anyone, anywhere in the world, who has an email
address.

More to the point, you can send quite large files as 'attachments' to an email. These files can be of any type so this
means you can send a very long document – an entire book if
required – to someone anywhere in the world for the cost of a
short local telephone call knowing that they will have it within
a few minutes. (However, be aware that some people do not
open attachments as they are capable of containing computer
viruses.)

The Internet – A Source of Information
Once you have set up an email account you will almost
certainly have access to the Internet. Some people love it
because it means they can find information about every
subject under the sun and held in virtually every country.
There is no doubt that the Internet is huge – so big that it is
impossible to imagine it. The problem is that, although the

information may be there, it may not be that easy to find what you want. The result is that this annoys some people who therefore prefer to use conventional methods instead.

A word of warning – even though the connection to the Internet is at local telephone rates, 'surfing' the net can create surprisingly large telephone bills.

The Internet – A Shop Window
We touched on this subject in Chapter 8 when we were talking about sales. It is possible to buy what is called a 'domain name' which is registered worldwide and then belongs exclusively to you. You can then design and maintain your web site yourself at your domain name (or arrange for a firm specializing in looking after web sites to do it for you). If someone links on to the Internet and calls up your domain address, they will see your web site. This site tells the world what you do in as much detail as you want.

As we saw before, if you don't know the exact name of the web site you are looking for, you can search for those that may interest you by using a 'search engine'. Let us say that you are making that exotic Old English drink, mead. This is a special product and you want to be able to sell it as far afield as possible. When your web site is designed it should include certain key words to ensure that your site is found as often as possible. In this case those key words could be 'mead', 'alcoholic' and 'drink'. There are probably others. You may decide to include 'traditional'. That would mean that anyone searching for, say, a traditional Welsh dresser would also find your web site. That may or may not be to your benefit but it is because search engines come up with a very wide range of sites that some people find making a search on the Internet irritating.

Some word processing programs and most desktop publishing programs can be used to create a web page and, in addition to those, there are a host of specific web page programs from which to choose. Again, however, you may be best advised to pay someone else to create your web page for you but do ask for a number of quotes and never just give the job to the first person who comes along.

The Internet – A Shop

Many organisations now offer their products for people to buy over the Internet by turning their web sites into shops. This means using a credit card as that is the only possible form of payment.

Some Internet 'shops' are highly reputable – the firm from whom we have been buying most of our stationery for the last few years now offers its goods on the Internet. However, it is only sensible to be very wary before giving your credit card details to an unknown organisation.

Whether or not your business would benefit from offering its goods in this way only you will know. It may not pay – one shop I know has found that, although they charge for post and packing, the time involved in dealing with the Internet sales is out of proportion to the profits they are making.

And finally . . .

What should you buy and from whom?

Hardware

Many computers are sold complete with a wide range of software. It is a mistake to think that this software is free as the price is, of course, built into the package. Ignore the software when you are comparing hardware prices.

Some chains and discount stores offer packages at very attractive prices – usually special deals with special discounts. At the other end of the scale is the small computer shop which builds equipment to the customer's specification and will load whatever software is required.

The former may well be cheaper but you are not likely to find that their after-sales service is very good. The latter can be a mine of helpful information and, because they tend to be run by enthusiasts, are often willing to spend time demonstrating various computers and explaining what different programs can do. Another advantage is that if you need to upgrade your hardware, this sort of shop can usually do so very economically. Most will also provide ongoing technical support.

Software

Deciding on exactly what software to buy and use is never easy. It has been said, with a good deal of truth, that the best program is the one you know best but if you are starting from scratch that is not very helpful.

The chances are that, whatever PC you buy, the operating system – the basic software which runs all other software – will be Microsoft Windows although the version may vary.

It must be said that if there is any reason to think that compatibility with other computer users could be important – in other words that you may want to be able to share information with others using file transfers – then sticking to Microsoft programs makes sense as they are more widely used than any others.

Although the salesman at one of the computer shops I telephoned dismissed training as not needed, I don't agree with him. Only those people who are very computer literate can sort things out for themselves within a reasonable time-scale. Some training is almost certainly needed and the fact is that you will find most training sources will base their teaching on Microsoft products.

From that you will understand that I suggest that the software package most suited to anyone setting out on their own would be Microsoft Office Professional Version which offers, together with those automatically included with the Windows operating system, all the programs you are likely to want (at least in the early years). This package includes Word (a word processor), Access (a database), Excel (a spreadsheet), Outlook (a contact management program) and Publisher (a desk top publisher) and, since all programs then come from the same stable, you will soon be able to understand how they work. Meanwhile, don't worry about the Internet – you will find the Windows operating system gives you all the software you need both to access the Internet and to use email.

INDEX

, setting up, 56 *et seq.*
, staff, 39–40, 52–53, 151
Credit, 104 *et seq.*
  limits, 106
  references, 106
Creditors, 69, 82–83, 103, 105

D
Database programs, 184–185
Debt finance, 122
Debtor, 103
Desktop publishing, 185
Direct costs, 38–39, 52
  mail, 93
Directories, 87–88
Directors, 67, 68, 69, 70
Disciplinary procedure,
  160–165
Dividends, 67, 80

E
Email, 186
Employment contract, 155 *et
  seq.*
Equipment, 57–58

F
Family, support from, 16–17
Filing, 118–119
Finance, 25–27, 120 *et seq.*
Fittings, 56–57
Fixtures, 57–58
Floppy disks, 178

G
Gearing, 121
Grants, 170
Gross profit, 39, 41
  , predicted, 42, 43

H
Health and Safety, 47, 166
Hoardings, 86

Home used as office, 100
Honesty, self-, 11, 13, 21
Humour, 15

I
Image, 145 *et seq.*
Ingoings, 56–57
Inland Revenue, 97 *et seq.*, 166,
  169
Insurance, 166–167, 168
Integrity, 15
Internet, 91, 186–188
Invoices, 148

J
Job cards, 109 *et seq.*
  description, 152
  title, 156

L
Law, company, 170
  , contract, 57, 168–169
  , employment, 167
  , tax, 169
Leaflets, 86–87
Legal advice, 57
Letterheads, 147–148
Letters, 179, 180
Life assurance, 171–173
Limited liability company, 67 *et
  seq.*, 78 *et seq.*, 101
Loans, 120 *et seq.*, 170–171
  , applying for, 125 *et seq.*
  , directors', 82–83
Logo, 146–147

M
Market research, 30 *et seq.*
  , target, 84–85
Marketing, 85 *et seq.*
Minimum wage, 54